POPE FRANCIS

Conversations with Jorge Bergoglio

POPE FRANCIS

Conversations with Jorge Bergoglio

SERGIO RUBIN AND
FRANCESCA AMBROGETTI

NEW AMERICAN LIBRARY

New American Library
Published by the Penguin Group
Penguin Group (USA) LLC, 375 Hudson Street,
New York, New York 10014

USA | Canada | UK | Ireland | Australia | New Zealand | India | South Africa | China
penguin.com
A Penguin Random House Company

Published by New American Library, a division of Penguin Group (USA) LLC.
Previously published in a G. P. Putnam's Sons edition.

First New American Library Trade Paperback Printing, October 2014

Originally published as *El Jesuita: Conversaciones con Jorge Bergoglio*, © 2010
Sergio Rubin and Francesca Ambrogetti
Copyright © Sergio Rubin and Francesca Amborgetti, 2010
Foreword and Appendix © 2010 Ediciones B Argentina SA
English translation © 2013 by Laura Dail Literary Agency, Inc.

REGISTERED TRADEMARK—MARCA REGISTRADA

NEW AMERICAN LIBRARY TRADE PAPERBACK ISBN: 978-0-451-46941-0

THE LIBRARY OF CONGRESS HAS CATALOGUED THE HARDCOVER EDITION AS FOLLOWS:
Francis, Pope.
Pope Francis: conversations with Jorge Bergoglio/Sergio Rubin and Francesca Ambrogetti.
p. cm.
"Originally published as *El Jesuita: Conversaciones con Jorge Bergoglio*, © 2010
Sergio Rubin and Francesca Ambrogetti."
ISBN 978-0-399-16743-0
1. Francis, Pope, 1936—Interviews. 2. Cardinals—Argentina—Interviews.
3. Jesuits—Argentina—Interviews. I. Rubín, Sergio. II. Ambrogetti, Francesca. III. Title.
BX1378.7.F73 2013b 2013015327
282.092—dc23

Printed in the United States of America
3   5   7   9   10   8   6   4   2

Designed by Claire Naylon Vaccaro

CONTENTS

PUBLISHER'S NOTE

On March 13, 2013, the former Cardinal Jorge Mario Bergoglio, archbishop of Buenos Aires, now Pope Francis, was elected to succeed Pope Benedict XVI, Joseph Ratzinger.

This book, first published in 2010, is the fruit of a series of journalistic interviews with Bergoglio when he was cardinal, consecrated by Pope John Paul II. They give insight into his core beliefs, his personal history, his wisdom, intellect, compassion, humility, and ultimately his humanity.

Here—in his own words—is an intimate look at the man who is now the leader of the Roman Catholic Church.

This is the life story of the current pontiff.

FOREWORD

As far as I know, this has to be the first time in two thousand years that a rabbi has written the foreword for a book about the thoughts of a Catholic priest. An act all the more significant when said priest is the archbishop of Buenos Aires and a cardinal consecrated by Pope John Paul II.

I saw the same sentence above, with which I begin these reflections, but with the names and titles reversed, when one of my own books was launched in 2006 with a foreword by then Cardinal Bergoglio.

It is not about an exchange of favors, but rather a sincere and accurate testimony to a profound dialogue between two friends for whom the search for God and the spiritual dimension that lies in every human being was and is a constant concern.

Interreligious dialogue, which acquired special significance after the Second Vatican Council, usually begins with a stage of "tea and sympathy" before moving on to the trickier subjects. With Bergoglio, there was no such stage. Our conversation began with an exchange of *terrible* jokes about each other's favored soccer teams and went immediately to the candor of sincere and respectful dialogue. Each of us expressed to the other his particular vision about the many subjects that shape life. There were no calculations or euphemisms, just clear and direct ideas. One opened his heart to the other, just as the Midrash defines true friendship (Sifrei Devarim, Piska 305). We sometimes disagree, but each always tries to understand the deep feeling and thoughts of the other. And with all that emerges from our shared values, those that come from the prophetic texts, there is a commitment that has been manifested in various actions. Beyond any interpretation or criticism that others might make, we walk together with our truth, with the shared conviction that the vicious cycles that degrade the human condition can be broken. With faith that the path of history can and should be changed, that the biblical vision of a redeemed world, as foreseen by the prophets, is not a mere utopia, but an achievable reality that needs only committed people to make it real.

This book is the life testimony of Bergoglio and was originally published with the title *El Jesuita* (The Jesuit), though I prefer to call him "the pastor." He dedicates it to the many who share his existential path and especially to his flock. The reader will repeatedly find expressions such as: "I have sinned . . . I was wrong . . . Such and such were my failings . . . Time or life has taught me . . ." Even in the tricky topics that come with Argentine reality, with the Church's actions during the dark years, and with his own actions, readers will hear stories told with humility, and they will see his constant thirst to understand and empathize with his neighbors, especially those who are suffering.

Some will disagree with his assessments, but beyond all possible criticism, everyone will agree on the considered nature, the humility, and the compassion with which he confronts every one of his topics.

Bergoglio's obsession, the leitmotif woven throughout the book, can be defined in these words: coming together and unity, understanding these as a state of harmony among men, in which everyone cooperates for both the material and the spiritual growth of everyone else, inspired by love.

Following biblical text, Bergoglio centers his reflections on the word "love," and refers to the following verses, among others: "You shall love the Lord, your God, with your whole heart" (Deuteronomy 6:5); "You shall love your neighbor as yourself" (Leviticus 19:18); "You shall treat the alien who resides with you no differently than the natives born among you; you shall love the alien as yourself" (Leviticus 19:34). "Love" is the word that defines the most exalted of man's feelings, and serves Bergoglio as a source of inspiration in the realization of his actions and in the forming of his message.

The reader will find in this book Bergoglio's vision with respect to the problems currently facing the Catholic Church, detailing without reservation and in clear critical language its failings. The teacher of faith, in accordance with the biblical worldview, should express his criticism to all members of the society in which he preaches, from the pulpit of the spirit, which is far away from all partisan interest.

In my own childhood, my father, an immigrant born in

Poland, used to take my brother and me to visit historical places. Leaving the Cabildo, he pointed out the image on the cathedral's façade. It represents the meeting of Joseph and his brothers, he said. I had heard about the anti-Semitism that my Polish ancestors experienced, and that image, decorating the top of a church, overwhelmed me with hope. A day will come, I thought, in which everyone will recognize their brotherhood with their neighbors.

I see this book and many of the stories in it as a tribute to that hope, a hope that we have shared as brothers for many years, that has enriched our spiritual lives, and that surely has brought us closer to that which blows the breath of life into every human being.

RABBI ABRAHAM SKORKA

Buenos Aires, December 23, 2009

INTRODUCTION

When Joseph Ratzinger was elected successor to Pope John Paul II and all the accredited journalists started their interviews in order to reconstruct what had happened in that papal conclave, they knew that the work would be more than difficult, almost impossible. Three oaths to keep the secret of what transpired in the Sistine Chapel, taken by the 117 voting cardinals, under penalty of excommunication if violated, seemed an insurmountable wall. Even so, one of the best-informed journalists covering the Vatican, Andrea Tornielli of the Italian daily paper *Il Giornale*, wrote an article published the day after the solemn announcement of the new pontiff—just as a daily newspaper of Argentina, *Clarín*, did simultaneously—that the Argentine Jesuit Jorge Mario Bergoglio had played an extraordinary role. Tornielli—

the journalist who initially had the most details—reported that in the second of the three ballots, Bergoglio received forty votes, an unprecedented number for a Latin American cardinal, making him the runner-up to Ratzinger, who in the end, of course, became Pope Benedict XVI.

Over time, other qualified observers echoed the same story. Among them, Vittorio Messori (the most translated Catholic journalist and writer over the last several decades, author of the celebrated book *Crossing the Threshold of Hope*, a long conversation with John Paul II, as well as a similar book, *The Ratzinger Report*, with then cardinal Ratzinger). "It is true that a conclave is a very secret thing, but one can always uncover something," said Messori. "Everyone agrees that in the first vote of the conclave, Cardinals Ratzinger and Bergoglio were practically tied." After clarifying that he is not a Vaticanist, but rather a student of Christian subjects, Messori cited "corroborating comments" to assert that Bergoglio had asked his peers to pass his votes to Ratzinger, the surest, almost obligatory candidate. "The thing is he valued having been the 'theological mind' of John Paul II, who best represented his continuity," Messori concluded.

Some observers believe that Bergoglio's chances grew

significantly after he passed another Jesuit, the embodiment of the progressive wing, Italian cardinal Carlo Maria Martini, who recused himself from the list of candidates due to health issues. But Martini was always too progressive for the conservative factions, the majority in the college of cardinals. It is also true that by the end of 2002, as the prestigious Vaticanist Sandro Magister wrote in the Italian weekly *L'Espresso*, if there had been a conclave at that moment, Bergoglio would have won "in a landslide" that would consecrate him pontiff. "Shy, reserved, of few words, he doesn't move a finger to campaign, but that is exactly what is considered one of his great assets," Magister said about the Argentine cardinal. He concluded: "His austerity and frugality, along with his intense spiritual life, are the personal qualities that increasingly elevate him to be 'popeworthy.'"

Magister's prediction was not far off. The Vaticanists—Tornielli among them—said that after the second vote, Bergoglio seemed overwhelmed by the number of votes he was receiving, and it was then that he decided to step aside and to ask that his votes go to Ratzinger—who, after him, had the most votes—because of all that Ratzinger embodied and to avoid that his own candidacy block the election and provoke a delay of the conclave that could negatively affect the Church's image. A delay could be read as a symptom of discord among the cardinals by a world that was watching them with enormous anticipation. In fact, members of the Holy See predicted in the days before the election that if Ratzinger were not elected quickly, they ran the risk of going to numerous votes until another cardinal got the two-thirds necessary. It's understandable, then, that Bergoglio did not want to carry such a heavy responsibility. In any case, most analysts concur that he played a pivotal role.

So, how to explain the "Bergoglio phenomenon"? We have to go back to the beginning of this century, because the Argentine cardinal was not well known among the high Church dignitaries of the five continents until extenuating circumstances placed him before their eyes around 2001. More precisely: in the weeks after September 11, 2001. The then archbishop of New York, Cardinal Edward Egan, was at the Vatican participating in an assembly of bishops from around the world and had to fly home to attend a ceremony in honor of the victims of the terrible attack on the Twin Towers. His role as the general counselor of the assembly, a key position, was filled by Cardinal Bergoglio, who left an excellent impression. All observers agree that this was the beginning of his international rise. He was the most voted for to date among the 252 Synodal fathers from 118 countries at that assembly of bishops to join the Post-Synodal Council, representing the Americas.

Bergoglio's prestige would be reconfirmed two years after the conclave, on the occasion of the Fifth General Conference of Latin American and Caribbean Bishops, which took place in Aparecida, Brazil. There, he was elected president of the strategic commission by a wide majority, charged with writing up the final summarizing document, a responsibility of even greater significance when you realize that similar conferences, like those of 1969 in Medellín, Colombia, and 1979 in Puebla, Mexico, produced declarations of enormous consequence about Catholicism.

Nor was that the only recognition Bergoglio earned at that event: the day he was to give Mass, his homily elicited enthusiastic applause. No other officiating priest was applauded throughout the three weeks of the conference. Witnesses say that many of the participants took advantage of the breaks to talk with the Argentine cardinal and even take pictures with him, as if he were a famous actor or illustrious athlete.

And yet anyone who has seen Bergoglio knows he is not a glamorous, TV-friendly figure. Nor is he a grandiloquent speaker of dramatic gestures; rather, he is soft-spoken, with profound content. Moreover, until being named auxiliary bishop of Buenos Aires in 1992, when he was fifty-five years old, he was a perfect outsider in the Church, not a career priest climbing up the ecclesiastical ladder.

At that time, he served as confessor in the residence of the Church of the Society of Jesus in Córdoba, where he had been stationed for about two years. It was the then archbishop of Buenos Aires, Cardinal Antonio Quarracino, who—impressed with his capabilities—chose him to be one of his auxiliary bishops. And one year later he made him principal, anointing him his general vicar. When Cardinal Quarracino's health began to deteriorate, he fostered Bergoglio as his successor (the pope named him assistant archbishop, or coadjutor archbishop, with the right to succession). When Quarracino died in 1998, Bergoglio became the first Jesuit to head the Buenos Aires curia.

By then, Bergoglio already had a strong influence over the city's clergy, especially the youngest. They liked his affable approachability, his sincerity, and his wise counsel. None of this would change with Bergoglio's arrival to the main seat of the archdiocese, the cardinal's residence. He would have a phone installed so that priests could call him at any hour. He would spend nights in any parish, attending to a sick priest if necessary. He would continue traveling by bus and subway, eschewing a car and driver. He would reject moving into the elegant archbishop's residence in Olivos, close to the presidential estate, and instead would remain in his austere room in Buenos Aires. He kept personally responding to calls, accepting visits, and keeping track of all his audiences and activities in a little rustic pocket notebook. And he would avoid social events, and preferred his simple dark clergyman's suit to the cardinal's cassock.

Speaking of his austerity, it is said that when it was announced he would be made cardinal in 2001, he didn't want to buy a new wardrobe, but preferred to tailor the clothes of his predecessor. And that as soon as he learned some of the faithful were planning to travel to Rome in order to attend the ceremony where Pope John Paul II would make him cardinal, he pleaded with them not to come, and to give the money for the trip to the poor instead.

It is also said that he made frequent trips to the shanty-towns of Buenos Aires, where during a chat with hundreds of men from the parish of Our Lady of Caacupé, in a slum in the Barracas neighborhood, a bricklayer stood up and said, clearly moved, "I am proud of you, because when I came here with my companions on the bus I saw you sitting in one of the last seats, like one of us. I told them it was you, but no one believed me."

From then on, Bergoglio had a permanent place in the hearts of those humble, suffering people. "We feel like he is one of us," they explained.

Many also remember from that time his attempt to stop a crackdown in the Plaza de Mayo during the protests of December 2001. When he saw police beating a woman from the window of his archbishop's residence, he picked up the telephone and called the Ministry of the Interior. The secretary of security took his call, and Bergoglio asked him to start differentiating between activists who were creating a disturbance and regular folks who just wanted to withdraw their savings from the bank.

This was the time that Bergoglio was rising in the national ecclesiastic ranks, and in 2004 he would be elected president of the Episcopal Conference (he was reelected in 2007). He led a moderate line, far from the powers that be and with marked social concern, that had been the majority for some time now in a traditionally conservative Church. It was a line that had been very critical of the neoliberalism of the 1990s and the prescriptions of the International Monetary Fund, which constantly sought repayment of the foreign debt on the basis of the sacrifice of those who had the least.

It is easy to detect in Bergoglio's pronouncements before the financial collapse at the beginning of the century his concern for the deteriorating situation in the country. His messages in the Te Deum on May 25, 2000—which became a kind of civic speech of great consequence—were eloquent. In 2000, when Fernando de la Rúa had been president for less than five months, Bergoglio said: "Sometimes I wonder if we aren't marching, in certain aspects of the life of our society, in a sad parade, and if we aren't putting a tombstone on our search as if we were walking toward an unavoidable destiny, doomed to impossible things, and we just resign ourselves to small illusions lacking hope. We must acknowledge, with humility, that the system has fallen into a period of dark shadow—the shadow of distrust—and that some of the promises and principles sound like a funeral procession, with everyone consoling the relatives, but nobody waking the dead."

After the worst of the crisis, in the *oficio patrio* Mass of 2003, before Néstor Kirchner, who had assumed the presidency just hours before, Bergoglio called for everyone to "carry the nation on their shoulders" to make the country great.

But it was his homily of the Te Deum Mass the following year that would end up having the largest political consequences. Among many other ideas, Bergoglio pointed out that Argentines "are quick to intolerance." He criticized "those who feel so included they exclude everyone else, those who are so clairvoyant they have become blind," and he warned that "copying the hate and violence of the tyrant and the murderer is the best way to inherit it." The next day, his spokesperson at the time, a priest named Guillermo Marcó, clarified that the archbishop's words were directed to the whole society, including the government and the Church itself, and that, in any event, "if the shoe fits, wear it." President Kirchner was highly annoyed and decided never to attend another Te Deum officiated by Bergoglio. And in an act not seen in two hundred years of Argentine history, he moved the *oficio patrio* out of Buenos Aires, to churches in various capitals of the province. Except for a chance occurrence—a tribute to the Pallottines massacred during the military dictatorship—Kirchner and Bergoglio never saw each other again.

The cardinal was often the target—especially during the 2005 conclave, in which he was one of the most likely papal candidates—of persistent journalistic attacks. Reporters accused him of turning over two Jesuit priests who'd been working in a slum to a marine command during the military dictatorship. The author of the report claimed that Bergoglio, who was at that time the leader of Argentina's Jesuits, was trying to push out the progressive members of the Church of the Society of Jesus.

Other observers thought just the opposite—that Bergoglio actually saved the lives of the two priests and circumvented an extreme crisis in his religious community. "It was a very difficult time for the Church of the Society of Jesus, but if he had not been at the forefront of it, the difficulties would have been much worse," said the order's two-time secretary of religious matters, Ángel Centeno.

To many leaders who visit him regularly, Bergoglio is a man of personal charm who captivates with his demeanor and shines with his guidance. To the regular people who for one reason or another come into contact with him, he is a simple, warm person, full of thoughtful gestures in things both big and small. For those who know his religious thinking intimately, he is the priest committed to getting the Church out among the people with a message of compassion and enthusiasm; the priest whose veneration would turn into a true phenomenon of popular devotion in Buenos Aires; the pastor who is ultimately respectful of orthodox doctrine and ecclesiastic discipline, but equally the owner of an understanding that is both modern and spiritually profound about the Church and living the Gospel in challenging contemporary society.

But who is this descendant of Italians, born in Buenos Aires in 1936? Who is this boy who graduated from high school as a chemical technician and at age twenty-one embraced his religious calling? Who is this Jesuit, ordained at age thirty-three, professor of literature and psychology, with degrees in theology and philosophy, speaker of several languages? Who is this religious man who was a teacher at the Colegio de la Inmaculada Concepción in Santa Fe, Argentina (1964–1965); provincial superior, from age thirty-six to forty-three, of the Company of Jesus in the country (1973–1979); and rector of the Colegio Máximo in San Miguel, Argentina (1980–1986)? Who is this priest, confessor of the community of the Colegio del Salvador of Buenos Aires (1986–1990), who in his first year took a six-month sabbatical in Germany, where he completed his thesis on the eminent theologian and Catholic philosopher Romano Guardini, who helped stoke the church reform that took shape in the Second Vatican Council?

Who is this teacher who brought Jorge Luis Borges to class and had him read his students' short stories? Who is this pastor convinced that the Church should go from "regulating faith" to "transmitting and facilitating faith"? Who is this religious minister who in a very few years went from a modest place in a Jesuit residence in the city of Córdoba to become archbishop of Buenos Aires, *cardenal primado* of Argentina, and president of the diocese? Who is this Argentine who lived an almost monastic life, and is now pope?

Despite the maxim that it is difficult to know what a Jesuit is thinking—and allowing a certain mysterious aura that goes with the personality—this book tries to answer those questions on the basis of a series of meetings with Cardinal Bergoglio that took place over the course of more than two years in the central office of the Buenos Aires archbishopric.

It wasn't easy to persuade him to do it. "Journalistic interviews are not my strength," he often says. (In fact, in our first meeting he agreed, initially, to discuss only his homilies and sermons.) When he finally agreed, he placed no conditions, although he showed a certain resistance to talking about himself in our efforts to show his human side and his spiritual dimension. And every session invariably ended with the cardinal's expressing doubt about the usefulness of the task: "Do you think anything I said might be helpful?"

There was never any attempt to exhaust the subjects that came up. Only to get a sense of the mind of this sensitive and yet also resolute and very sharp man, who had already become an important key to the Church in the world. His responses reflect a country in constant crisis, a Church plagued with challenges, and a society that searches, often unconsciously, to satisfy its thirst for transcendence. To men and women who want to find meaning in their lives, to love and to be loved, and to find happiness, his answers are, in sum, an invitation to think with your gaze upon the most high.

SERGIO RUBIN

FRANCESCA AMBROGETTI

POPE FRANCIS

Conversations with Jorge Bergoglio

CHAPTER I

Grandma Rosa and Her Fox-Fur Coat

The heat was intense that January morning of 1929, when the Bergoglio family first set foot on the Buenos Aires docks. Their arrival did not go unnoticed. Heading up the group was an elegant woman clad in a fox-fur coat, which, while glamorous, was nonetheless utterly inappropriate for the stifling, muggy Buenos Aires summer. This was not some outlandish whim on the part of the wearer: in the lining of her garment, Rosa Bergoglio carried the proceeds from the sale of the assets the family had owned in Italy, which they needed to embark on their new life in Argentina. The deal had taken considerably longer than expected, a state of affairs that in all probability ended up saving their lives, for the Bergoglios had tickets to travel from Genoa some time before on board the tragically famous ship *Principessa Mafalda*. Had they boarded that ship, it almost surely would have been their final voyage, since the vessel's hull was pierced and it sank off the north coast of Brazil, taking hundreds of lives down with it. In the end, the family set sail on the *Giulio Cesare*.

They came from the north of Italy, from a village called Portacomaro in the Piedmont region. They were leaving behind a continent that had yet to heal from the ravages of the First World War, with deep fears that another war could break out at any moment, a Europe plagued by economic hardship. They arrived in a country in which such turmoil and tension were a distant memory, one that held the promise of seemingly untold job opportunities, better pay, the chance of an education for all, and considerable social mobility. In other words, they arrived in a land of peace and progress. Unlike most immigrants who, upon arrival, put themselves up in the dockside Hotel de Inmigrantes, the Bergoglio family kept traveling to the capital of the Entre Ríos province, where most of the rest of their family anxiously awaited their arrival.

His family's roots, their journey to the country, his parents' recollections, and his childhood exploits were all on the agenda of our first meeting with Bergoglio, arranged in the visitors' chambers of his Buenos Aires archbishopric, set to be the venue for all of our meetings. No sooner had we asked our questions than the stories came flooding back to him: the narrow escape from the voyage of the *Principessa Mafalda*, the family's arrival at port (his future father among them, twenty-four years old at the time), his grandmother and her fox-fur coat, their beginnings in the capital of Entre Ríos.

Why did your family set sail for Argentina?

Three of my grandfather's brothers had been here since 1922 and had started a paving business in Paraná. That was where they built the four-story Bergoglio palazzo, the first building in the city to have an elevator. It had a very pretty turret, much like the one on the El Molino café in Buenos Aires, which was later removed. The brothers lived one to a floor. But the crisis of 1932 left them penniless; they

were even forced to sell off the family tomb. One
of my great-uncles, the president of the
company, had already passed away from cancer,
another one started out fresh and made a go of
things, and the youngest headed for Brazil.
My grandfather asked for a two-thousand-peso
loan and bought a warehouse. My father, who
was an accountant and worked on the
administrative side of the company, helped him
out by distributing merchandise until he found
work at another company. They started over from
scratch with the same optimism with which they
began. I think that testifies to their strength of
character.

Were they struggling in Italy?

No, not really. My grandparents owned a café, but
they wanted to go to Argentina in order to be
near their siblings. There were six of them in all,
and two stayed behind in Italy, one brother and
one sister.

That notion of keeping the family together is very European and, above all, very Italian.

That's true. In my case, I was the one who took the traditions most to heart, as I was taken in by my grandparents. My mother had my first brother when I was thirteen months old; there are five of us in all. My grandparents lived around the corner, and, in order to help out my mother, my grandmother would come fetch me in the morning, take me to her house, and bring me back in the evening. My grandparents spoke Piedmontese to each other, and I picked it up from them. They loved all of my siblings, needless to say, but I had the privilege of partaking in the language of their memories.

How much nostalgia did your elders feel?

I never detected a shred of nostalgia in my father, which meant he must have felt it, since he denied it for some reason. For example, while he never spoke to me in Piedmontese, he did with my grandparents.

It was something he kept under wraps, something
he'd left behind; he preferred to look to the future.
I remember one time I was replying to a letter from
one of my father's teachers who had written to me at
the seminary. My Italian was rusty, and when I asked
my father how to spell a word, I noticed his
impatience. He replied abruptly, as if to bring the
conversation quickly to an end, and took his leave.
It was as if, over here, he had no wish to talk about
back home, although he would with my
grandparents.

Some people say that Buenos Aires faces away from
the river because it was built mostly by immigrants
who suffered the wrench of leaving home and
uprooting their families, and they preferred to turn
the city to face the Pampas, which represented the
future.

The origin of the word "nostalgia"—from the Greek
nostos, homecoming, and *algos*, pain—has to do with

a yearning to return, the *Odyssey* speaks of this. What Homer does through the story of Ulysses is light the way back to the bosom of the earth, the maternal bosom of the earth from which we sprang. I believe that we have lost nostalgia in its anthropological sense. But we have also lost it when it comes to teaching—for example, nostalgia for the home. When we put our elders in nursing homes with a couple of mothballs in their pockets as if they were an overcoat, in a certain sense our nostalgic side has failed us, since being with our grandparents means coming face-to-face with our past.

Something every immigrant can identify with.

Absolutely. Every immigrant, not just the Italians, has to deal with this tension. One great master of nostalgia, the German poet Friedrich Hölderlin, has a very beautiful piece he dedicated to his grandmother the day she turned seventy-two. It

begins, "You have lived many things . . . Oh dear
mother . . ." and ends with: "May the man
not let you down on what he promised as a child."
I remember this very well, as I feel a special
devotion to my grandmother, for all that she
gave me in the first years of my life. Speaking
of Piedmontese, I am also a great admirer of
Nino Costa, who penned very romantic
verses.

From memory, and with great feeling, Bergoglio recited
a poem in dialect about Piedmontese immigrants, before
going on to translate one stanza:

Ma 'l pi dle volte na stagiun perdüa
o na frev o 'n malör del so mesté
a j'ancioda 'nt na tumba patanüa
spersa 'nt un camp-sant foresté.

But most times a lost season
or a fever or a misfortune at work

nails them in a bare tomb

lost in a foreign cemetery.

He concluded: "The poetic nostalgia expressed here by Costa lies in having loved, but having been unable to return. There is also a great deal of reflection about the nostalgia of migration in the book *Il Grande Esodo* (The Great Exodus) by Luigi Orsenigo."

How did your parents first meet?

They met at Mass in 1934, in the San Antonio chapel in the Buenos Aires neighborhood of Almagro, where they lived. They got married the following year. She was the daughter of a Piedmontese woman and an Argentine descended from Genoese people. I recall one of those great-uncles very well; he was a rascally old man, and he taught us to sing some rather risqué ditties in Genoese dialect. That explains why the only things I can say in Genoese do not bear repeating.

Did you have fun with your parents?

Yes, we played *brisca* and other card games. My
father played basketball at the club in San Lorenzo;
he'd take us along sometimes. With my mother, we
listened to the operas broadcast on Radio del Estado
(now Radio Nacional) at two o'clock on Saturday
afternoons. She'd sit us down around the radio and,
before the opera got under way, she'd explain what it
was about. Listening to *Otello*, she'd say, "Listen—
he's going to sing a very beautiful song now." The
truth is that two o'clock on Saturday afternoons with
my mother and my siblings, enjoying music, was a
wonderful time.

**Did you behave yourselves? It's not easy for a young
boy to connect with opera.**

Sure . . . well. Sometimes we'd drift off halfway
through, but she'd hold our attention, keeping up
her explanations throughout the performance.

During *Otello*, she'd warn us, "Listen up: now he kills her." These are the things I recall from my youth: the presence of grandparents, whose role has gradually fallen by the wayside in society but who now, thanks to the financial crisis, are reemerging, because they're needed to take care of the kids. And above all, I remember my mother and father sharing with us, playing . . . cooking . . .

Cooking?

Let me explain: My mother became paralyzed after giving birth to her fifth child, although she recovered over time. But during that period, when we got home from school we'd find her seated, peeling potatoes, with all the other ingredients laid out. Then she'd tell us how to mix and cook them, because we didn't have a clue. "Now put this in the pot and that in the pan . . ." she'd explain. That's how we learned to cook. We can all cook veal escalopes, at least.

Do you cook now?

No, I don't have time. But when I lived in the
Colegio Máximo in San Miguel, there was no cook
on Sundays, so I'd fix something for the other
students.

Are you a good cook?

Well, no one ever died . . .

CHAPTER 2

"You Should Start Working . . ."

When he finished elementary school, Jorge's father called to him and said, "Now that you're starting secondary school, you should also start working; I'm going to find you something over vacation." Jorge, barely thirteen years old, looked at him a little disconcerted. At home they lived comfortably off the pay of his father, who worked as an accountant. "Though we had nothing to spare, no car, and didn't go away for the summer, we still never wanted for anything," Bergoglio says. In any case, he agreed obediently.

Soon he was working in a hosiery factory that was served by the accounting firm his father worked for. For the first two years, he worked as a cleaner. In his third year, he was given administrative work to do, but during the fourth year, his career path and the time he dedicated to it took a turn.

As he attended a technical school that specialized in food chemistry, he managed to find work in a laboratory, where he would work from seven a.m. to one p.m. He barely had an hour to eat lunch before attending classes, which lasted until eight p.m.

More than half a century later, he believes that that job—which he continued after he finished his schooling—ended up being very valuable to his training.

"I'm so grateful to my father for making me work. The work I did was one of the best things I've done in my life. In particular, in the laboratory I got to see the good and the bad of all human endeavor," he says. In a wistful tone, he adds: "I had an extraordinary boss there, Esther Balestrino de Careaga, a Paraguayan woman and communist sympathizer. Years later, during the last dictatorship, both her daughter and son-in-law were kidnapped; later she herself was abducted together with the missing Franciscan nuns, Alice Domon and Léonie Duquet, and murdered. She is now buried in the church of Santa Cruz. I loved her very much. I remember that when I handed her an analysis, she'd say, 'Wow, you did that so fast.' And then she'd ask, 'But did you do the test or not?' I would answer, 'What for?' If I'd done all the previous tests, it would surely be more or less the same. 'No, you have to do things properly,' she would chide me. In short, she taught me the seriousness of hard work. Truly, I owe a huge amount to that great woman."

This recollection serves as a jumping-off point for a new topic of discussion: work.

Over the course of your life as a priest, you must have encountered many unemployed people. What has your experience been?

> Definitely, there have been many. They don't feel like they really exist. No matter how much help they might have from their family or friends, they want to work, they want to earn their daily bread with the sweat from their own brow. The thing is, at the end of the day, work anoints a person with dignity. Dignity is not conferred by one's ancestry, family life, or education. Dignity as such comes solely from

work. We eat with what we earn, we support our families with what we earn. It doesn't matter if it's a little or a lot. If it's more, all the better. We can own a fortune, but if we don't work, our dignity plummets. A typical example is that of the immigrant who arrives with nothing, struggles, works hard, and achieves the "American Dream." But they have to be careful, because their children or grandchildren might become spoiled if they are not instilled with a good work ethic. Because of that, immigrants do not tolerate lazy children or grandchildren: they make them work. May I tell you something that comes to mind?

Of course.

I remember the case of a Buenos Aires family of Basque origin. It was the 1970s, and the son was very involved in social protest. The father was a dairy farmer. The two of them had serious ideological differences. As they both had a lot of respect for a certain elderly priest, they invited him to dinner to resolve their conflict. The priest went along, listened to them patiently, and in the end, like the wise old man he was, he told them, "The problem is that both of you have forgotten the cramps." Father and son, confused, asked him, "What cramps?" And the priest replied, pointing at both of them, "The cramps of your father and of your grandfather, from getting out of bed every day at four in the morning to milk the cows!"

Of course, sacrifice makes you see things in a different light.

For the moment, let's move away from fruitless theorizing. The father had devoted himself to, let's say, the establishment, and the son had strongly embraced a different ideology, because both had forgotten about work itself. Work opens a door to realism, and in itself constitutes a clear mandate from God: "Be fertile and multiply; fill the earth and subdue it." That is to say, be masters of the earth: work.

*But it's the worst for everyone who wants to work
but can't.*

What happens is that the unemployed, in their hours
of solitude, feel miserable because they are not
"earning their living." That's why it's very important
that governments of all countries, through the
relevant ministries and departments, cultivate a
culture of work, not of charity. It's true that in
moments of crisis one must have recourse to aid to
be rescued from an emergency, like the Argentines
experienced in 2001. But after that, they have to
cultivate sources of work because, and I never tire of
repeating this, work confers dignity.

*But the scarcity of work poses an enormous
challenge. Some people are even talking about
"the end of work."*

Well . . . fewer people working means fewer people
consuming. Man intervenes even less in production,
but at the same time, who will buy the products? It

seems a little shortsighted. I don't think we are exploring alternative forms of work. For example, some countries, knowing that they cannot provide work for everyone, reduce the number of working days or hours with the idea that people will have more "fulfilling leisure time." But the first step is creating sources of work. We must not forget that the first social encyclical, *Rerum Novarum*, was born in the shadow of the Industrial Revolution, when conflicts were beginning and there were no leaders emerging with the capacity to create alternatives.

On the other hand, there's the problem of too much work . . . Do we need to rediscover the meaning of leisure?

In its true sense. Leisure has two meanings: that of idleness, and that of gratification. Together with a culture of work, there must be a culture of leisure as gratification. To put it another way: people who work must take time to relax, to be with their families, to enjoy themselves, read, listen to music, play a sport. But this is being destroyed, in large part, by the elimination of the Sabbath rest day. More and more people work on Sundays as a consequence of the competitiveness imposed by a consumer society. In these cases, we can see the other extreme: work ends up dehumanizing people. When work does not yield to healthy leisure, to restorative rest, then it enslaves you, because then you are not working for dignity, but to compete. This vitiates the intention of work.

And, of course, it undermines family life.

Because of that, one of the questions I always ask young parents during confession is whether or not they spend time playing with their children. Sometimes, they're surprised; they don't expect this kind of question, and they admit they've never asked themselves that. Many go to work before their children wake up and come home after they've gone to sleep. And on weekends,

overwhelmed by tiredness, they don't pay attention
to them like they should. Healthy leisure means that
both mother and father play with their children.
Healthy leisure has to have this recreational
element, and there is something profoundly wise
in this. The Book of Wisdom states that God
Himself, in His wisdom, rested. On the other hand,
leisure as idleness means the negation of work.
As Tita Merello sang in a *milonga*: "Hey, lazybones,
get out of bed."

**But it's not easy to find that balance. One can easily
go "off track."**

That's true. The Church has always maintained that
the key to the social question is work. The working
man is at the center. Today, in many cases, this is not
so. You can easily get cast aside if you don't yield to
what's expected. You become a thing, no longer
considered a person. Over the past few decades, the
Church has denounced the dehumanization of work.
Remember that one of the principal causes of suicide

is failure at work in the face of fierce competition. Because of this, you cannot look at work purely from a functional perspective. What's at the core is neither profit nor capital. Man is not for work; rather, work is for man.

CHAPTER 3

"You Are Imitating Christ"

For three terrible days, he struggled between life and death. At one point, delirious with fever, twenty-one-year-old Jorge Bergoglio embraced his mother and desperately asked her, "Tell me, what's happening to me?"

She didn't know how to answer him, because the doctors were bewildered. Eventually, they diagnosed him with severe pneumonia. They had found three cysts, and after he stabilized and a safe time had passed, he had to undergo an excision of the upper part of his right lung.

Every day, saline was pumped through his body to clean out his pleura and scar tissue. A chest tube was connected to a drainage system, producing a trickle of water. The pain was enormous.

Bergoglio didn't care for the usual platitudes that people kept telling him, things like "This will pass" or "Won't it be nice when you're back home?" But one visitor broke away from the clichés and truly comforted him.

It was a nun whom he had remembered ever since she prepared him to receive his First Communion, Sister Dolores. "She said something that truly stuck with me and made me feel at peace: 'You are imitating Christ,'" he recalled.

It was very clear to us that, for him, the sister's idea was an excellent lesson in how to confront pain in a Christian manner. And from the detail he went into with his story, his tone of voice slower and more deliberate than usual, we could see how facing death at such a young age had left a mark on him. Ever since, he has lived with a pulmonary deficiency that, even though it doesn't seriously affect his life, does demonstrate his human limitation. This episode certainly strengthened his discernment of what is important and what is trivial in life. And it strengthened his faith. Could it be that pain can be a blessing if it is endured in a Christian manner? Bergoglio put it this way: "Pain is not a virtue in itself, but you can be virtuous in the way you bear it. Our life's vocation is fulfillment and happiness, and pain is a limitation in that search. Therefore, one fully understands the meaning of pain through the pain of God made Christ."

To illustrate how we should face different situations, he recalled a dialogue between an agnostic and a believer in a novel by the French writer Joseph Malègue. In it, the agnostic says that for him, the problem was that Christ was not God, whereas for the believer, the problem was what would happen if God had not created Christ, or rather, if God had not come to shed light on the path. "The key," Bergoglio reflected, "is to understand the cross as the seed of resurrection. Any attempt to cope with pain will bring partial results, if it is not based in transcendence. It is a gift to understand and fully live through pain. Even more: to live life fulfilled is a gift."

But does the Church focus too much on pain as the path to getting close to God, and too little on the joy of the resurrection?

It's true that at times, the question of suffering has been overemphasized. I'm reminded of one of my favorite films, *Babette's Feast*, where you see a typical case of taking prohibitive limits to the extreme. The characters are people who live a form of exaggerated puritan Calvinism, to the point where they experience the redemption of Christ as a negation of the things of this world. When the novelty of freedom arrives in the form of an abundant meal, they all become transformed. In truth, this community didn't know what happiness was. They lived their lives crushed by pain. They were devoted to the gray side of life. They feared love.

But the main symbol of Catholicism is a crucified Christ dripping blood . . .

The exultation of suffering in the Church depends a great deal on the era and the culture. The Church has represented Christ according to the cultural environment of the time. If you look at Eastern icons, Russian, for example, you realize they have very few images of a sorrowful crucifixion. It's more common to see the resurrection. On the other hand, if we look at the Spanish Baroque period or the

icons of Cuzco, Peru, we find images of Christ with
His patience torn to shreds, because the Baroque era
emphasized Jesus' passion. *White Crucifixion* by
Marc Chagall, who was a Jewish believer, is not
cruel, but hopeful. Pain is depicted there with
serenity. To my mind, it's one of the most beautiful
things he painted.

*You can't deny that over the course of two
millennia, the Church has highlighted martyrdom
as a path to sainthood.*

We should clarify something: to speak of martyrs
means speaking of people who bore witness until
the end, until their death. To say that "my life is a
martyrdom" should mean "my life is testimony." But
nowadays, the idea has become associated with the
gruesome. Nevertheless, for some witnesses, the
word becomes synonymous during their final stretch
of life with giving one's life to faith. The term, if
you'll forgive me the expression, has been belittled.
Christian life is bearing witness with cheerfulness, as

Jesus did. Saint Thérèse of Lisieux said that a sad
saint is a holy sadness.

**Bear witness with cheerfulness, even when the
Church encourages penitence and sacrifice as
a form of expiation?**

Of course, yes. You can fast and put yourself
through other forms of deprivation and continue
your spiritual progress, without sacrificing peace
and cheerfulness. But be careful not to fall into the
heresy of Pelagianism, a form of self-sufficiency,
according to which you can consecrate yourself if
you do penitence, and therefore, everything becomes
penitence. In the case of pain, the problem is that on
certain occasions, it's mishandled. In any case, I am
not very fond of just theorizing at people who are
experiencing tough times. It reminds me of the
passage in the Gospel about the Samaritan woman
who had five failed marriages and could not come to
terms with it. And when she met Jesus and started
to talk about it in theological terms, the Lord

brought her down to earth. He assists her with her problem, she faces up to the truth, and He doesn't alienate her with theological deliberation.

And as for yourself, how do you handle a life brought to an end by a cruel illness?

I stay silent. The only thing that occurs to me is to remain quiet and, depending on the trust they have in me, to take their hand. And to pray for them, because both physical and spiritual pain are borne from within, where no one can enter; it entails a great deal of solitude. What people need is to know that someone is with them, loves them, respects their silence, and prays that God may enter into this space that is pure solitude. I remember another film in which an innocent woman is condemned to death and taken to death row. As she was a businesswoman connected with the world of jazz, the prison guard meets her with blaring music. The woman cries out, begging the guard to switch off the song. She doesn't want artificiality, only her solitude. The scene also illustrates society's recurrent desire to camouflage death.

In what way?

The situation shows the ridiculousness of certain hedonistic cultures that go so far as to make up corpses, or even lay them out in a funeral parlor. This is not common, but it is done in some places. There is also the matter of certain cemeteries that act as museums, works of art, beautiful places, all to conceal the drama which lies beneath them.

Incidentally, do you ever think of your own death?

For a while now it's been a daily companion of mine.

Why is that?

I'm over seventy years old and the thread of life I have left on the reel isn't long. I'm not going to live another seventy, and I'm starting to consider the fact that I have to leave everything behind. But I take it as something that's normal. I'm not sad. It makes me want to be fair with everyone always, to sign the final flourish. Mind you, it's never occurred to me to make a will. But death is in my thoughts every day.

CHAPTER 4

The Spring of Faith

For him, it was a great gift that sneaked up on him unnoticed. It was September 21 and, like many young people, seventeen-year-old Jorge Bergoglio was getting ready to go out with his friends for Students' Day. But he decided to start the day by visiting his parish church. He was a practicing Catholic who attended the Buenos Aires church of San José de Flores.

When he arrived, he met a priest he'd never seen before. The priest conveyed such a great sense of spirituality that he decided to confess to him. He was greatly surprised when he realized that this was not just another confession, but a confession that awakened his faith. A confession that revealed his religious vocation, to the point where he decided not to go to the train station to meet his friends, but instead went home with a firm conviction. He wanted to—he had to—become a priest.

"Something strange happened to me in that confession. I don't know what it was, but it changed my life. I think it surprised me, caught me with my guard down," he recalls more than half a century later. Bergoglio now has his own theory about that mystery: "It was the surprise, the astonishment of a chance encounter," he says. "I realized that they were waiting for me. That is the religious experience: the astonishment of meeting someone who has been waiting for you all along. From that moment on, for me, God is the One who *te primerea*—'springs it on you.' You search for Him, but He searches for you first. You want to find Him, but He finds you first." He adds that it was not only the "astonishment of the encounter" which revealed to him his religious vocation, but the compassionate way in which God called him—in such a way that, over time, it became a source of inspiration for his own ministry.

However, his entry into the seminary was not immediate. "The subject ended there," he states. He went on to finish his schooling and continued to work at the nutrition analysis laboratory, not confiding his decision to anyone. Even though he was certain of his religious vocation, he spent the following years in a crisis of maturity that led him to spend time in solitude. Bergoglio says that it was a "passive solitude," the kind that one suffers for no apparent reason, or due to crisis or loss, as opposed to an "active solitude," which one experiences when facing transcendental decisions. The experience taught him to live in harmony with solitude. Finally, at the age of twenty-one, he decided to enter the seminary and ended up opting for the Jesuits.

Why did you choose to become a Jesuit priest?

To tell the truth, I didn't really know which path to take. What was clear to me was my religious vocation. After studying at the archdiocesan seminary of Buenos Aires, I ultimately entered the Society of Jesus because I was attracted to its position on, to put it in military terms, the front lines of the Church, grounded in obedience and discipline. It was also due to its focus on missionary work. I later had an urge to become a missionary in Japan, where Jesuits have carried out important work for many years. But due to the severe health issues I'd had since my youth, I wasn't allowed. I guess some people would have been "saved" from me here if I had been sent over there, right? [Laughter.]

How did your family react when you told them you wanted to be a priest?

I told my father first, and he took it very well. More than well: he was happy. The only thing he did was ask me if I was absolutely certain about my decision. He later told my mother, who, being a good mother, already had an inkling. But her reaction was different. "I don't know, I don't see you as . . . You should wait a bit . . . You're the

eldest . . . Keep working . . . Finish university,"
she said to me. The truth is, my mother was
extremely upset.

*You could say you made the right decision when
you chose which of the two to give the news to
first . . .*

I definitely knew my father was going to understand
me better. His mother was a very strong religious
role model for him, and he had inherited that
religiousness, that fortitude, as well as the great pain
that comes from being uprooted. On the other hand,
my mother experienced it as a plundering.

What happened next?

My mother didn't come with me when I entered the
seminary; she refused. For years, she didn't accept
my decision. It's not that we were fighting. I would
go home to visit, but she would never come to the

seminary. When she finally accepted it, she did so by putting some distance between us. When I was a novitiate, in Córdoba, she came to visit me. Don't get me wrong: she was a religious woman and a practicing Catholic; she just thought that everything had happened too fast, that it was a decision that required a lot of time to think over. But she was rational. I remember her kneeling before me after the priestly ordination ceremony was over, asking for my blessing.

Perhaps she thought the priesthood wasn't for you, that you wouldn't get very far . . .

I don't know. What I do remember is that when I told my grandmother, who had already known but pretended not to, she replied, "Well, if God has called you, blessed be." And immediately she added, "Please never forget that the doors to this house are always open, and no one will reproach you for anything if you decide to come back." That attitude, which we might call a supportive attitude for someone who is about to undergo a very important test, seemed like a vital lesson to me in how to treat people who are going through a period of transition in their lives.

In any case, your decision was not a hasty one. You waited four years before entering the seminary.

Let's say that God left the door open for me for a few years. It's true that I was, like the rest of my family, a practicing Catholic. But my mind was not made solely for religious questions. I also had political concerns, though I never went beyond simple intellectualizing. I read *Our Word and Proposals*, a publication by the Communist Party, and I loved every article ever written by Leónidas Barletta, one of their best-known members and a renowned figure in the world of culture, and that helped me in my political education. But I was never a communist.

*To what extent do you believe it was your own
decision, and to what extent was it a "choice
of God"?*

Religious vocation is a call from God to your heart,
whether you are waiting for it consciously or
unconsciously. I was always very moved by a breviary
that said Jesus beheld Matthew with an attitude that,
translated, would be something like "by having
compassion and by choosing" (*miserando atque
eligendo*). That was precisely the way I felt that God
saw me during that confession. And that is the way
He wants me always to look upon others: with much
compassion and as if I were choosing them for Him;
not excluding anyone, because everyone is chosen by
the love of God. "By having compassion and by
choosing" was the motto of my consecration as a
bishop, and it's one of the centerpieces of my
religious experience: service in the name of
compassion and the choice of people based on a
suggestion. A suggestion that could be colloquially
summarized like this: "Look, I ask for you by

name, I choose you, and the only thing I ask is that
you let yourself be loved." This is the suggestion I
received.

**Is that why you say God always te primerea, "springs
it on you"?**

Of course. God defined himself to the prophet
Jeremiah as the branch of an almond tree. And the
almond tree is the first to flower in spring.
Primerea—it is always first. John said: "In this
is love: not that we have loved God, but that he
loved us . . . We love because he first loved us." For
me, if the religious experience doesn't have this
measure of astonishment, of surprise, if this
compassion is not sprung upon you—then it's cold, it
doesn't draw us in completely; it's a different kind of
experience that doesn't bring us to a transcendental
plane. Though we all know that living this kind of
transcendentalism today is difficult, due to the dizzy
rhythm of life, the fast pace of change, and the lack
of a long-term view. However, oases are very

important to the religious experience. I've always been impressed by something Ricardo Güiraldes wrote in *Don Segundo Sombra*: that his life was marked by water. When he was a boy, he was like a lively little stream among the pebbles; when he was a man, a tempestuous river; and as an old man, a peaceful oasis.

Do you have any suggestions for the creation of these oases?

Spiritual retreats are artificially created oases, where everyday rhythm pauses and gives way to prayer. But remember! What is artificial about them is the creation of space, not the retreat itself. The kind of spiritual retreat where you listen to a cassette of religious behaviors with the aim of being stimulated into a response won't work—it doesn't soothe the soul. The encounter with God must come surging from within. I must put myself in the presence of God and, aided by His Word, go forward in what He desires. What is at the heart of

all this is the question of prayer. It is one of the
points that, in my opinion, must be approached with
the most courage.

The lack of oases, is that just about a lack of time,
or is it also a question of believers putting their
spiritual needs aside?

They get put aside until you slip on a banana peel
and fall. Be it an illness, a crisis, a disappointment,
something you'd overenthusiastically planned that
didn't work out . . . I remember something I once
witnessed in an airport that left me very sad. It
happened at the point when all the passengers, from
economy and from first class, mingle around the
baggage carousel, waiting for their suitcases. For a
moment, we are all equal and all waiting for
something; the carousel equalizes us. Suddenly, one
of the travelers, a well-known older businessman,
started to get impatient because his suitcase hadn't
arrived. He didn't hide his frustration at all, and his
expression seemed to say, "Don't you know who I

am? How can they make me wait like I'm just anyone?" What first surprised me was that an older person could be so impatient.

Young people, who have their whole lives ahead of them, are usually the most impatient.

Thinking of the life he had led, of his desire to live the myth of Doctor Faustus, wanting to stop the clock at thirty years old—it made me sad to see this person who didn't know how to appreciate the wisdom of age. Instead of aging gracefully like a fine wine, he'd gone sour like a bad one. Ultimately, it made me sad to see someone with so much success in some ways, yet with such an essential failure. You can have everything, live in abundance, have all the bells and whistles, and yet still get so upset if your suitcase is delayed. Deep down, he's just one person alone, forming part of a group of people to whom the Lord gives the possibility of rejoicing in Him and with Him, without needing to be a priest or a nun; but by making life revolve around himself, he winds up as vinegar instead of a well-aged wine. The image of well-aged wine works for me as a metaphor for religious maturity and human maturity, which go together. If, as a human, one remains stuck in adolescence, the same will happen in the religious dimension.

In your opinion, what should the experience of prayer be like?

In my view, prayer should somehow be an experience of giving way, of surrendering, where our entire being enters into the presence of God. It is there where a dialogue happens, the listening, the transformation. Look to God, but above all feel looked at by God. Sometimes the religious experience in prayer occurs to me when I pray aloud with the rosary or the psalms. Or when I joyfully celebrate the Eucharist. But the moment when I most savor the religious experience, however long it may be, is when I am before the tabernacle. At times, I allow myself to fall asleep while sitting there, looking at it. I feel as if I were in someone else's hands, as if God were taking me by the hand. I think you have to reach the transcendental otherness of the Lord, that the Lord is everything, but He always respects our freedom.

How do you examine your life and your ministry before God?

I don't want to mislead anyone—the truth is that I'm a sinner who God in His mercy has chosen to love in a privileged manner. From a young age, life pushed me into leadership roles—as soon as I was ordained as a priest, I was designated as the master of novices, and two and a half years later, of the province—and I had to learn from my errors along the way, because, to tell you the truth, I made hundreds of errors. Errors and sins. It would be wrong for me to say that these days I ask forgiveness

for the sins and offenses that I might have
committed. Today I ask forgiveness for the sins and
offenses that I did indeed commit.

What is it you most reproach yourself for?

What hurts me the most are the many occasions
when I have not been more understanding and
impartial. In morning prayers, in supplications, I
first ask to be understanding and impartial. I then
continue asking for many more things related to my
failings as I travel through life. I want to travel with
humility, with interpretative goodness. But I must
emphasize, I was always loved by God. He lifted me
up when I fell along the way, He helped me travel
through it all, especially during the toughest periods,
and so I learned. At times, when I have to confront a
problem, I make the wrong decision, I behave badly,
and I have to go back and apologize. All of this does
me good, because it helps me to understand the
mistakes of others.

One might think that a believer who'd achieved the rank of cardinal would have things very clear . . .

That's not the case. I don't have all the answers. I don't even have all the questions. I always think of new questions, and there are always new questions coming forward. But the answers have to be thought out according to the different situations, and you also have to wait for them. I confess that, because of my disposition, the first answer that comes to me is usually wrong. When I'm facing a situation, the first solution I think of is what not to do. It's funny, but that's how it works for me. Because of this, I have learned not to trust my first reaction. When I'm calmer, after passing through the crucible of solitude, I come closer to understanding what has to be done. But no one is exempt from the solitude of decision-making. You can ask for advice, but in the long run, it's you who must decide, and you can do a great deal of harm with the decisions you make. One can be very unfair. Because of that, it's so important to commend yourself to God.

CHAPTER 5

Educating
from Conflict

I t was his favorite subject and he knew it perfectly, but they had sent him to the exam for not having finished an assignment, so he knew passing it would not be easy. He knew they weren't going to make it easy for him. It was a premonition that proved correct the moment he approached the examiner's desk. "Now, then, little boy . . . which question do you choose?" asked one of the examiners. "None!" his teacher answered for him. The teacher added, amid some confusion: "He's going to talk about all the material." The third examiner at the table, as if to break the tension, ironically noted, "Well, at least that means there's nothing you've studied in vain."

From the back of the room, there was a murmur, and one of his classmates predicted, "They're going to crucify him." However, the examiners at the table didn't interrupt the young man's presentation, nor did they ask any questions. Finally, his teacher said, "Strictly speaking, you should get a ten, but we will award you a nine. This is not to punish you, but it's so you always remember that what matters is fulfilling your duty every day; performing systematic work without letting it become routine; building things up brick by brick, rather than in a fit of improvisation that seduces you so."

The teacher was Jorge Bergoglio and the student Jorge Milia, who recounts this story in his memoirs about his youth, *De la Edad Feliz* (From the Happy Age), written forty years later. "I never forgot that lesson, which I keep in mind even today, and I didn't think they could've treated me more fairly," recounts Milia in his heartfelt book, in which he describes the years he spent studying at the Colegio de la Inmaculada Concepción in Santa Fe, Argentina. It was a Jesuit educational establishment that, in the mid–twentieth century, enjoyed a singular reputation: many traditional families from Santa Fe, other provinces, and even bordering countries sent their sons to study there.

It was at this school that Father Bergoglio had his first experience as a teacher, which he then continued at the Colegio del Salvador in Buenos Aires. "Before entering the seminary, I'd studied chemistry and thought I'd teach some science subjects, but no, they entrusted me with teaching psychology and literature. I had studied psychology when I'd taken philosophy, so I found that easy, but as for literature, even though I liked it a lot, I had to spend the whole summer preparing," says Bergoglio.

He recalls that he tried to teach classes that were "as flexible as possible: I would choose an author and an era, but if anyone preferred someone else from the same period, or even from a different one, I'd let them go for it. For example, when I taught *El Cid*, one student told me he preferred the poem by Antonio Machado based on this work, and I told him to 'go right ahead' with Machado. The boys liked to find risqué things in Machado and competed to see who could find the most. I let them," he says.

In his book, Milia remembers this teaching method: "Throwing us in at the deep end with the poem of El Cid was like making us tilt at the windmills of Don Quixote, but it was never as bad as we feared: the good thing about

Bergoglio was there were never any closed doors. Anyone who wanted to explore the monument that is the Spanish language was able to do so in all the necessary detail, without euphemisms or restrictions."

Bergoglio also tells us that to inspire the students, he made them write stories, and on a trip to Buenos Aires, he showed the stories to none other than Jorge Luis Borges. "He liked them and encouraged us to publish them, promising he'd write the prologue," he says. And so it came to be: they were published under the title *Original Stories*.

Milia, who wrote one of the stories, describes the experience with great excitement, the same excitement he felt the day when Bergoglio brought Borges himself to teach a class at Santa Fe, as he had done with other authors.

Milia also collected memories from his former fellow students, one of whom said of their teacher: "He didn't look like a fighter, but there was something about him that alerted us to a particular type of character. Cheerful, with a youthful face, he had a short-lived nickname of *carucha*—'the face,' but it was nothing more than that: a façade. Inside, he was a methodical and steadfast man, the 'commando' of Christ in the Society of Jesus, which had promised to turn us out well." Milia also describes how, after that scholarly period and Bergoglio's departure to new pastures, "I always found in him, far beyond the role he played as a friend, a teacher, and a priest, a man who is aware of his duty and his mission to bear witness to faith, and always with his deep sense of humor."

Sentiments that were mutual: "I loved them very much," Bergoglio wrote in the book, recalling those students. "They never were, nor are they now, indifferent to me, and I never forgot them. I want to thank them for all the good they did me, particularly for the way they taught me how to be more a brother than a father."

After some memories and anecdotes about his teaching experience, we dive into the proposed topic of this discussion: education. We begin by mentioning that while experts claim the Argentine school system is falling behind, they also believe that a society facing so much change and uncertainty needs an institution with one of the most trustworthy reputations to remain a solid point of reference. Schools are one of the few places where there is an attempt to maintain the principle of authority. We begin by asking him:

How can schools find the tricky balance between being anchored in the past, which can be a necessary point of reference, and the need to educate their students about a different world, to envision a future they will one day be part of?

Let's talk about the student and then go on to expand it to the school. It's often said that in education, you have to bear two things in mind: the safety zone and the danger zone. You can't base education solely on the safety zone, nor only on the danger zone: you have to keep things in proportion—not balanced, but in proportion. Education always means an imbalance. You start to walk when you notice something's missing, but if there's nothing missing, you don't walk.

So what would be the healthy educational balance?

You have to walk with one foot in the safety zone, or, rather, in the material that students have already learned and assimilated, where they feel safe and comfortable. And with the other foot, venture into the danger zones, which must be proportional to the safety zones, to the individual, and to the social climate. By doing so, you turn this danger zone into a safety zone, and step by step, you advance their education. But without danger, you can't advance, nor can you do so with pure danger.

Does this bear any relation to what you call "shipwrecked culture"?

Partly yes, because the person who is shipwrecked is faced with the challenge of surviving through his creativity. He can hope that someone will come rescue him, or he can begin his own rescue himself. On the island where he lands, he has to start to build a hut. He can use the planks from the shipwreck, but also whatever new elements he finds around him. It's the challenge of taking on the past, even though it no longer floats, and using the tools offered by the present to face the future.

Can you give us a specific example?

> Yes. I know of some schools in Hamburg where they
> tried to educate through spontaneity and freedom,
> without fixed rules, without relying on the safety
> zone, and they failed. This safety zone, incidentally,
> must also be provided within the family.

Some people say that, nowadays, adolescents, young
people, find it very difficult to accept an education
that comes from adults who don't have any kind of
security. The boy doesn't accept authority, because
the adult who is meant to be giving a sense of
authority transmits doubt, from being part of a
society that, in itself, constantly fills us with doubt.
So where should we go to find at least some
certainty, and thus transmit a sense of security?

> The starting point has to be the great existential
> truths. For example, the concept of doing good and
> avoiding evil, which is one of the most elementary
> moral certitudes. There are also cultural certitudes

and social certitudes. But you must have the great existential certitudes made flesh in the coherence of life, and from there, you can move forward.

How can bearing testimony influence this?

A lot. A certitude is not just advice, an intellectual conviction, or a saying. It is also a testament, an agreement among what you think, what you feel, and what you do. It's fundamental that one thinks what one feels and does; feels what one thinks and does; and does what one thinks and feels. You must use the language of the head, the heart, and the hands.

Can you give an example?

Yes, of course. While some people may be culturally limited in terms of their education, they may still embody three or four certitudes in a coherent way, and by doing so and bearing witness, they educate their children very well. I am reminded of the example of Paraguayan women, the most glorious

women in the Americas. At the end of the
nineteenth century, they found themselves with
the dilemma of either giving in and accepting defeat
or saying, "My country has lost the war, but it will
not lose history." There were eight women for every
one man at the time, and yet they continued to
educate in order to build a faith, a culture, and a
language.

Perhaps schools should identify permanent values,
and separate them from values that belong to a
certain culture or social custom. Identify them and
not confuse them, so as to avoid invalidating the
former when the latter are inevitably replaced over
time by other cultures and customs.

Exactly. It would be ridiculous to speak today in the
language of Cervantes, yet the Spanish values
contained in his work absolutely endure. Today, we
in Argentina can find our own cultural values in, for
example, literary works such as *Martín Fierro* and

Don Segundo Sombra. Or, rather, we find the same values expressed in another way. In any period of change you can use the image of the shipwrecked man that I mentioned earlier: there are things that no longer serve us, the transitory things, as well as other values, which can be expressed in a new way. And, of course, there are practices that are later considered to be intolerable and utterly repugnant. Let us consider the great cultural shipwreck that was slavery. Before slavery was abolished, it was considered normal that men could be bought and sold at market.

That said, when it comes to deciding their children's education, do you believe parents really prioritize the teaching of values even when they're looking for religious schools? And do you believe that schools are now at their peak in this regard?

I think that, in general, parents who have more choices allow themselves to be taken in by the

promotional aspects offered to their children: "This
school will equip them with more useful tools for
the future," they say, thinking about its computer
studies or language departments, for example, but
they don't put as much consideration into the
question of values. Beyond the importance of having
a good curriculum, this demand means some schools
choose to focus on promoting the functional,
forgetting things as vital as the developmental
aspects. Indeed, religious educational institutions in
general, and Catholic ones in particular, are not
exempt from this risk.

*When speaking of values, it's inevitable to invoke
the old figure of the teacher who set an example,
who laid down the rules, who knew how to
understand students and established a human
relationship with each one.*

I think education is overly professionalized. Of
course, it's essential to change with the times, and a

professional attitude is very healthy. But that shouldn't come at the expense of forgetting to consider the student three-dimensionally.

Can you give us an example of a specific incident that has touched you?

Yes, I remember, when I was a vicar in Flores in the early 1990s, a girl at a school in the neighborhood of Villa Soldati became pregnant. It was one of the first times something like this had happened in that school. People had a number of opinions about how to deal with the situation; some were contemplating expulsion, but no one took it upon themselves to think about how the girl must be feeling. She was scared of people's reactions and wouldn't let anyone come near her. Until one young teacher, a man who was married with children, whom I respect very much, offered to talk to her and work out a solution. When he saw her during recess he gave her a kiss, took her hand, and gently asked, "So you're going to be a mother?" and the girl started crying uncontrollably. This gesture of closeness allowed her to open up and talk about what had happened, and it allowed them to arrive at a mature and reasonable response. It meant that not only did she not have to give up her schooling or face life with a child on her own, but they also avoided that, in the eyes of her classmates—something that had been another worry—she be seen as a heroine for getting pregnant.

So he found the solution through acceptance, not through rejection?

Exactly. What the teacher did was take the initiative to talk to her. He ran the risk of having the girl just respond with "And what's it to you?" but he had his great humanity in his favor, and he sought to approach her with a loving attitude. If you try to educate using only theoretical principles, without remembering that the most important thing is the

person in front of you, then you fall into a kind of
fundamentalism. This does nothing for children
because they can't absorb lessons that aren't
accompanied by a life's testimony and a degree of
closeness, and sometimes with nothing but theory,
after three or four years, it comes to a head and they
act out.

*Do you have a formula for how to avoid succumbing
to cold, aloof severity when teaching values, while
still not falling into the trap of the kind of teaching
that just tries to get students on your side, allowing
the kind of relativism where anything goes?*

I don't have a formula. But maybe this will help.
I usually tell priests that when they are in the
confessional, they should be neither too severe nor
excessively indulgent. The disciplinarian is one who
applies the rules without a second thought. "The law
says this, and that's that," he says. The lenient one
sweeps it aside. "It's fine, whatever, life is like that,

move on," he says. The problem is that neither of the two pays attention to the person in front of them; they take it from on high. "And so, Father, what should we do?" they ask me. And I tell them, "Be compassionate."

Does the current state of schooling in Argentina help in this respect?

Not at all. Teachers are poorly paid and have just enough to get by. What's more, in the classrooms there are too many children and teachers can't spend enough time with every one of them. But that's not a recent problem. What's more, the pact of education is broken. The parents, teachers, students, unions, the state, and religious denominations are no longer fighting for the same side, as they ought to be, and the one who pays the price is the child. Concerted action is needed.

There's a statistic that claims 68 percent of teacher absences are for psychological reasons. More than anything, they feel overburdened by the way many parents neglect their role, shifting many of their responsibilities to the schools.

That's true. Not long ago, I heard some members of the Vicarage of Education of the archdiocese discussing the issue of children who are desperate to talk to their teachers; evidently, there's a lack of conversation at home and they feel neglected. It's important to spend time talking to children, to keep your ears open, even though we often think they're being silly. But among the hundred things they say, there's one thing that is unique, and deep down they're looking for something: for you to pay attention to their particularities, to say to them, "You're okay." I'm very interested in the age of "why," when children are waking up to the world around them and feel very insecure. At this stage, the learning curve is steep, not on an intellectual level but in the sense of learning their place in a world that scares them. So what they need is not necessarily an explicit answer, but just a look from their fathers or mothers that makes them feel safe; they need to talk so they feel looked at, identified. This happens later on, too.

What's more, teachers often feel undermined by parents who don't allow them to say anything bad to their children . . .

When we were young, and this isn't necessarily something that's better or worse, if we came home with a note, we'd be in for a tongue-lashing. But these days many parents blame the teacher who wrote that note, and they go speak with them to defend their little ones. This takes authority away from the teachers; the child no longer respects them. And when you take away authority, you remove a space for growth. Authority comes from the Latin *augere*, meaning "to make grow." To have authority is not to be an oppressor. Oppression is a distortion of authority. When exercised correctly, authority implies creating a space where a person can grow. Anyone with authority is capable of creating a space to grow.

Perhaps the meaning of the word has become distorted . . .

Clearly. It has become synonymous with "I'm in charge here." It's strange, but when the parent or teacher has to say, "I'm the one in charge here," or "I'm better than you here," it's because they've already lost authority. And then they have to reinforce it with that word. To claim that one has the "upper hand" implies that they no longer have it. And having the "upper hand" doesn't mean to order and impose; it means to serve.

CHAPTER 6

Playing Tarzan

The then auxiliary bishop of Buenos Aires, Jorge Bergoglio, closed the file that he was working on in his office and looked at the time. He was expected at a retreat in a convent on the outskirts of Buenos Aires, and he had just enough time to catch the train. Even so, he first walked the short distance to the cathedral. As he did every day, he wanted to pray before the Holy Sacrament, even if just for a few minutes, before continuing his hectic activity.

Inside the temple he felt relieved by the silence and the freshness, in contrast to the heat of a torrid summer afternoon. As he was leaving, a young man, who appeared to have mental health problems, approached him and asked to confess. Bergoglio had to make an effort to hide the annoyance he felt at the delay this would cause.

"The young man must have been around twenty-eight years old, and he talked as if he were drunk, but it was apparent that he was probably under the effect of some psychiatric medication," recalls Bergoglio. "So I," he continues, "the witness of the Gospel, the one who practices apostleship, told him, 'Right now you'll just have to go to a father and confess with him, because I've got something to do.' I knew that the priest wouldn't be in until four, but I thought, since the man was medicated, he probably wouldn't notice the delay, and I rushed out. But after a few steps, I felt a tremendous sense of shame; I returned and told him, 'The father is going to be late; I will hear you confess.'"

Bergoglio still recalls how, after hearing his confession, he took the man before the Virgin to ask her to care for him, and then finally went on his way, thinking of the train, which by now would have departed. "But when I reached the station, I discovered that service had been delayed and I could catch the same train. When I returned, I didn't head home but went straight to my confessor, because what I had done was weighing on me. I told myself, 'If I don't confess, tomorrow I won't be able to celebrate Mass with this on my mind.' Ultimately, it was a situation in which there was no room for efficiency or efficacy."

Bergoglio is strict when it comes to reproaching himself on this matter. "At that moment, I was playing Tarzan," he says. He explains that "it was the middle of January, and the archbishop of Buenos Aires, who at the time was Cardinal Antonio Quarracino, was traveling, and I, as general vicar, was in charge of the diocese. In the morning, I attended to issues of the curia, and at two in the afternoon, I was to go to Once railway station to catch the train to Castelar, where we were giving spiritual exercises to some nuns. I had," he insists, "an attitude of superiority—put another way, I was sinning. But I didn't realize it. In some ways, I was saying to myself, 'Look how good I am, how great I am, how many things I can do.' Pride affected my attitude."

In another meeting, Bergoglio recounts this episode to us after having mentioned a phrase that he has repeated to himself often: "travel through patience." What does he mean by this concept? He responds so quickly and so emphatically, barely letting us finish the question, that it becomes clear that, without realizing it, we have touched on something important.

"It's a phrase that dawned on me over the years while reading a book by an Italian author with a very suggestive title, *Teologia del Fallimento*, or *A Theology of Failure*, which sets out how Jesus entered into patience. By reaching the limit," he adds, "by confronting the limit, patience is forged. Sometimes life forces us not to 'make,' but to 'suffer,' enduring—from the Greek *ypomeno*—our own limitations as well as the limitations of others. Traveling with patience," he explains, "is knowing that what matures is time. Traveling with patience is allowing time to rule and shape our lives."

It's impossible to avoid considering the current situation of the country in this light, and we ask him if he thinks Argentines often seem incapable of exercising patience. Instead of slowly building their future, they look for immediate results, they try to find the "shortcut," the quickest way . . . "To take that last example," he answers us, "it's a matter of the dialectic between the journey and the path. Everybody loves a shortcut, not just Argentines. A shortcut," he says, "has the element of an ethical trap: avoiding the road and opting for the path. You see this in the small things, too, whenever we avoid making the effort."

Do you think that patience needs to be learned?

Yes. To travel in patience means accepting that life is a continuous learning experience. When you're young, you believe you can change the world, and that is good, that's the way it should be. But later, when you seek this change, you discover the logic of patience in your life and the lives of others. To travel in patience is to make peace with time, and allow for others to open up your life for you. A good father, like a good mother, is one who intervenes in the life of his child just enough to demonstrate guidelines for growing up, to help him, but who later knows when to be a bystander to his own and others' failures, and to endure them.

An example of this could be the parable of the prodigal son.

That parable has had a great effect on me. The son asks for his inheritance, the father gives it to him, then he goes, he lives his life how he wants, and returns. The Gospel says that the father saw him coming from afar. So he must have been at the window, to see if he'd ever return. In other words, he'd been waiting patiently.

This reminds me of when we were boys and we used to fly a kite in the little plaza on the way home. There was a moment when the kite was doing figure eights and started to descend; to avoid that, you were supposed to not pull on the string. 'Let it go, it's kicking!' those of us who knew would yell out. Flying a kite is similar to the attitude we need regarding a person's growth: at some point you have to let the string go slack. In other words: you have to give things time. We have to know the right time to draw the line. But on the other hand, we also have to know when to step back and act like the father in the parable, who let his son go and waste his fortune to have his own experience.

And with ourselves?

It's the same. We must allow ourselves to travel
in patience. Especially when we have failed or
sinned, when we realize that we've gone too far,
when we acted unfairly or shamefully. I did not travel
in patience that afternoon in the cathedral, because I
had to catch the train, but in the end I caught it
anyway, because it was delayed. It was a sign from
the Lord, who was telling me: "See, I am the one
who will sort out the story." So often in life we ought
to slow down and not try to fix everything at once!
To travel in patience means these things: it's giving
up the presumption of wanting to solve everything.
You have to make an effort, but understand that one
person cannot do everything. You have to put the
myth of efficiency into perspective.

Does patience help when it comes to pain?

More than ever. We have to remember that we
cannot be born into this world without pain. It's not

only women who suffer when bringing a child into the world, but all people must go through painful moments in order to grow. Pain is something that produces fruitfulness. Don't get me wrong, this isn't a masochistic attitude. It's just accepting that life creates limits for us.

Among other believers, Christians must lead the field in embracing patience, because they trust in the will of God . . .

Careful, remember that Christian patience is not quietist or passive. It's the patience of Saint Paul, which means enduring, bearing history on one's shoulders. It's the archetypal image of Aeneas, who, as Troy burned, took his father on his shoulders (*et sublato montis genitore petivi*), took his history on his shoulders and walked toward the mountain in search of the future.

CHAPTER 7

The Challenge of Going Out to Meet People

The day arrived when we were going to discuss specific religious questions: aspects of the Catholic doctrine, and ways the Catholic Church should move forward in its work today. But where to begin? The subject is too vast. We certainly didn't plan to exhaust it, not in the least, just to sound out Bergoglio's thoughts on some critical questions and hot topics in society. One of the first things that often comes up at the dinner table or conversations in cafés is people's disengagement from religion and, in particular, from the Catholic Church, in many cases attracted instead by proposals from evangelical communities. The phenomenon of a kind of "privatization" of faith is well known, a religious existence without any kind of ecclesiastic intervention—"I believe

in God, but not in priests," as the popular saying goes—
accepting certain beliefs and discarding others, and paying
little attention to practices of worship and lay commitments.

Generalizations are flawed by nature. The current situation is not the same in the Catholic Church in Europe, which
is experiencing serious trouble, as it is in some regions of Africa or Asia, which are undergoing significant expansion. Nor
is the varied status of Catholicism in the United States the
same. But Latin America, though it also contains its nuances,
might make for a good synthesis of a culmination of current
challenges, based on a substratum of Catholicism that is
weathered yet undeniable. The lack of concrete facts about
changes in the number of believers certainly complicates the
analysis. But it is not too bold to state—based on estimates
made by experts of the Latin American Episcopal Conference (CELAM, or Consejo Episcopal Latinoamericano)—
that in the last few decades, the Church lost somewhere
around 20 percent of its believers, and the leakage toward
other religions or none at all must be even greater.

In line with the current state of the rest of the region, the
percentage of Catholic believers in Argentina has also fallen,
although by less than the average across Catholicism as a

whole. According to a survey carried out by the National Scientific and Technical Research Council (CONICET, or Consejo Nacional de Investigaciones Científicas y Técnicas) and four national universities in early 2008, 76.5 percent declared themselves Catholic, while the national census of 1960—the last to record information on religious affiliation—showed that 90.5 percent were members of this religion. Even though a survey cannot measure up to a census, comparing the two figures leads to estimates that over four decades, the Catholic Church has lost 14 percent of believers. Put another way, three out of every four Argentines is Catholic (although attendance at Sunday services—as in many other countries—is at barely 10 percent of believers).

Cardinal, is the Church doing well at its job?

I'm going to speak of the Church in Argentina, which is what I know best. The pastoral guidelines for the New Evangelization, issued by the bishops in 1990, began to point to the importance of a "friendly welcome." The temptation that we clergy can fall into is being administrators and not pastors. This means that when people come to the parish to request a sacrament or anything else, they are not always met by the priest but by the parish secretary, who, from time to time, can turn out to be a bit of a shrew. There used to be a secretary in the diocese whom the congregation called "the tarantula." The problem is that these kinds of people not only scare people away from the priest and the parish, but also from the Church and from Jesus. We must not forget that for many people, the parish on their way home from work is the "gateway" to the Catholic religion. That is very important.

As opposed to many evangelical communities, where there is friendliness, closeness, people know one another by name. Nor do these communities wait for people to come to them; they go out and seek them.

It's essential that Catholics—by which I mean the clergy as much as the laypeople—go out to meet people. A very wise priest once told me that we were facing a situation that is the complete opposite of the

Parable of the Lost Sheep. The shepherd had ninety-nine sheep in his flock and went out to search for the one that was lost; we have one in the flock and ninety-nine that we are not searching for. I sincerely believe that in this day and age, the most basic thing for the Church is not to reduce or limit the requirements or make this or that easier, but to go out and seek people, to know people by name. Not just because this is its mission, as the Gospel proclaims, but because if it isn't done, then it will do us harm.

In what way?

If the Church limits itself to the work in its parish and lives shut up in its community, then the same thing will happen to it that happens to a person who shuts himself in: it will atrophy, physically and mentally. Or it will deteriorate like the inside of a locked room, mold and damp spreading everywhere. The same thing happens to a self-referential Church as to a self-referential person: it becomes paranoid. It's true that if you venture out onto the street, the

same thing could happen to you as could happen to
anyone: you could have an accident. But I prefer an
injured Church to a sick Church a thousand times
over. In other words, I think a Church that limits
itself to the administrative, that only watches over its
small flock, is a Church that, in the long term,
becomes sick. The shepherd who locks himself in is
not a true pastor for his sheep, but just a
"hairdresser" for sheep, putting in their curlers,
instead of going out to seek others.

How can this be applied in big cities like Buenos Aires?

A while ago, an article by an Italian journalist said
that religious sociologists had discovered that a
parish has a zone of influence with about a seven-
hundred-meter radius. In Buenos Aires, the distance
between one parish and the next is typically around
two thousand meters. For this reason, I once
suggested to the priests that we rent out a garage,
and if we find a willing layperson, we send him there

to spend time with people, give religious instruction, and even give Communion to the sick or to those who are willing. A parish priest told me that if we did that, the believers wouldn't come to Mass anymore. "Is that so!" I exclaimed. "Do you mean to say that you have so many coming to Mass at the moment?" I asked. "No," he replied. The act of getting out there to meet people also means getting out from ourselves a bit, getting away from the enclosure of our own opinions to see if they might also be an obstacle, if they are somehow closing the door to God, and also focusing on listening. In any case, the priests know their duties.

You mentioned this is also pertinent for laypeople . . .

Absolutely. The problem, as the Italian journalist noted, is clericalization: priests often clericalize the laity, and the laity want to be clericalized. It's a matter of complicit sinning. But the laity has potential that is not always fully taken advantage of.

We think that baptism is enough when it comes to meeting people. I am reminded of some Christian communities in Japan that went without priests for over two hundred years. When the missionaries returned, they found them all baptized, catechized, and legitimately married by the Church. What's more, they realized that every person who had died had had a Catholic funeral. Faith was kept intact by the gifts of grace that gladdened the lives of the laity, who only received baptism but then continued to live their apostolic mission.

It's also true that the Church used to rely on a more stable society in terms of religion, with "captive believers" who had "inherited" their faith and who, at least to some extent, followed the dictates of the Church. Today, the "religious market" is more competitive and people are more questioning of religious orientations.

A few months ago, in Buenos Aires, we introduced some guidelines for the promotion of baptism that

echoed that very sentiment. I'd like to read what we
spoke of in the presentation: "The Church, coming
from an era when it was favored by the cultural
model of the time, became accustomed to the fact
that its authority was offered and open for those who
came to us, for those who sought us. This worked in
an evangelized community. But in the current
climate, the Church needs to transform its
framework and pastoral roles, focusing more on the
missionary side. We cannot remain in the 'patronage'
mind-set, which passively waits for 'the client' or
parishioner to come, but instead we need a structure
that enables us to go where we are needed, where
the people are. We need to go to the people who
want us but won't come to outdated institutions and
customs that don't respond to their expectations or
sensibilities. We have to take a creative look at how
we make ourselves present in social spheres, making
our parishes and institutions places that initiate these
spheres. We must overhaul the inner workings of the
Church to go to God's faithful people. Pastoral
conversion calls us to go from being a Church that is

the 'regulator of the faith' to one that is a
'transmitter and facilitator of the faith.'"

This all requires a change in mentality . . .

It requires a missionary Church. A high-ranking
member of the papal curia, who had been a parish
priest for many years, once told me that he knew
even the names of the dogs in his congregation. And
I don't think that's due to his good memory, but to
what a good priest he is. "Even though they're
making you cardinal, never stop being who you are,"
I told him. And he never did. There are so many
examples. Cardinal Agostino Casaroli, who became
secretary of state of the Vatican, used to go to a
juvenile detention center every weekend. He
always went by bus with his cassock and his
briefcase. Another Jesuit who enjoyed visiting
prisons told me that when visiting a particular
prison, he was surprised by the apostolic zeal of a
certain priest who taught religious instruction and

even played games with the young offenders. He
was so impressed by him that he started to confess
to him. Over time he discovered that it was . . .
Casaroli!

It can't be easy to avoid the risk of becoming a bureaucrat . . .

But it's essential to avoid it. Shortly before dying,
John XXIII had a long meeting with Casaroli, and
when Casaroli was about to retire, John Paul II
asked him to continue visiting the boys in
prison. "Never leave them," he advised him.
John XXIII was also a priest who went out onto the
street. As the patriarch of Venice, he would usually
go out around eleven to Saint Mark's Square to
perform the so-called "rite of the shadow," which
entailed sitting in the shade of a tree or outside a
bar, drinking a glass of white wine, and spending a
few minutes speaking with parishioners. He did this
like any Venetian, and then continued with his job.

For me, this is a true pastor: someone who goes out to meet people.

Of course, it's not just a question of going out to meet people, but also of getting them excited. Don't you think they might also be scared off by some sermons, the kind filled with reprimands?

Of course. People leave when it doesn't get through to them, when they can't recognize it in the little things, when they can't pick it up. But they also leave when they don't take part in the joy of the message of the Gospel, in the joy of Christian living. This is not just a problem for priests, but also for laypeople. It is not a good Catholic attitude to go looking solely for the negative, what separates us. That is not what Jesus wants. Doing so not only makes our message distorted and frightening, but it also implies a lack of acceptance, and Christ accepted everything. We are redeemed only by what we accept. If you don't accept that there are people with different opinions, even opposing opinions, opinions that you don't share, and if you don't respect them or pray for them, you will never redeem them in your heart. We must not let ideology trump morality.

The Bible has the Ten Commandments, but also the Beatitudes. Benedict XVI once stressed that the Catholic religion is not a "catalog of prohibitions."

I'm very much in agreement. This is very clear in his encyclicals about charity and hope. What's more, when Benedict XVI went to Spain, everyone thought he would criticize the administration of Prime Minister José Luis Rodríguez Zapatero because of his differences with the Catholic Church on various matters. Someone even asked him if he had spoken with the Spanish authorities on the subject of marriage between homosexuals. But the pope stated that no, he spoke with them about positive matters and the rest would come later. In some way, he was saying that first you have to emphasize the positive,

the things that unite us; not the negative, the things
that divide us. You must prioritize the connection
between people, the path we walk together. After
that, addressing the differences will be easier.

*As a counterpoint, doesn't there exist a growing
tendency toward "religion à la carte"? Choosing the
priest you like the most, the precepts that
inconvenience you the least?*

It's a very common tendency, one that responds
to modern consumerism. Some might choose a
Mass on the basis of how the priest preaches. But
after two months, they say the choir isn't right and
then switch again. It's a case of reducing religion to
the aesthetic. It's browsing the display rack in the
religious supermarket. It's religion as a consumer
good, which I believe is very much linked to some
kind of vague theism as part of the New Age
movement, a mixture of personal satisfaction,
relaxation, and "well-being." You see this
especially in the big cities, but it's not just a

phenomenon among educated people. In the
poorer areas and the slums, on occasions they'll
turn to a particular evangelical pastor, because "he
gets me."

But is it such a serious problem if people stick with
the celebration that most moves them, or the priest
who most enthuses them?

Or whatever best suits our ideology, because within
this "religion à la carte," people sometimes also
make religious choices based on ideology. I choose
this or that Mass because the officiating priest has
"good doctrine" or because this or that priest is
"more open" or "more progressive."

Coming to the question, I'd say the serious issue
would be that all this indicates a lack of a personal
connection with God, of an authentic religious
experience. This is what I believe is at the heart of
"religion à la carte." I believe that you have to
reclaim the religious event as a movement toward an
encounter with Jesus Christ.

Incidentally, what is your opinion of so-called
liberation theology?

> It was an interpretative consequence of the Second
> Vatican Council. And, like all consequences of an
> internal change of direction within the Church, it
> has its good points and its bad, its restraints and its
> excesses. As you'll recall, at the time, John Paul II
> charged then Cardinal Ratzinger with studying
> liberation theology, which resulted in two
> instructions, two successive reports, which described
> it and also noted its limitations (one of which is the
> appeal to the Marxist interpretation of reality), but
> also showed its positive aspects. In other words, the
> position of the Church in this area is broad.

Do you mean to say there wasn't a mass
condemnation of it, as is often popularly thought?

> Not at all. Nor did it speak of a condemnation of
> certain aspects in a legal sense, but a criticism. The
> preferential option for the poor was a strong message

of the post-Council. It's not that it hadn't announced this before, but the post-Council emphasized it. Catholicism's greatest concern regarding the poor in the sixties was the issue of fertile ground that could give rise to any kind of ideology. This could detract from what the Church asked of the Second Vatican Council and has maintained ever since: to espouse the right path in responding to an absolutely inescapable evangelical demand, one that is central, such as concern for the poor, and which, in my view, appears fully formed in the bishops' conference in Aparecida.

So, do you believe that there were liberation theologians who took the wrong path?

There were missteps. But there were also thousands of pastors, be they priests, religious men or women, young, adult, or old laypeople, who committed themselves to the Church and are the honor of our work, the source of our joy. The danger of an ideological infiltration was disappearing, insofar as

what was growing was our awareness of the treasure
of our people: popular piety. For me, the greatest
thing written about popular religion was in the
apostolic exhortation of Paul VI, *Evangelii
Nuntiandi*, and it is repeated in the Aparecida
document, in what I believe to be its most beautiful
part. So the more that pastoral agents discover
popular piety, the more that ideology falls away,
because they get close to people and their problems.

*So up to what point should the Church involve itself
in contemporary matters, such as denouncing
injustices, without falling into improper
politicization?*

I think the word "partisan" comes closest to the
answer I want to give. It's a matter of concerning
oneself not with partisan politics, but with the great
politics born of the Commandments and the Gospel.
Denouncing human rights abuses, situations of
exploitation or exclusion, or shortages in education
or food, is not being partisan. Catholic social

teaching is full of denunciations, yet it is not partisan. When we come out and say things, some accuse us of playing politics. I say to them, yes, we are playing politics in the Gospel sense of the word, but not the partisan sense.

CHAPTER 8

The Risk of Degrading the Religious Message

Cardinal Bergoglio came up with a definition almost in passing that is certainly relevant: "Currently the Church chooses not to reduce or discard its tenets or to make this easier or make that easier, but to go out and look for people." He must surely have been referring to an opinion that is voiced more and more often in the broader society and even among many of the faithful: that Catholicism ought to modify some of its ideas and rules to "be more in sync with the times," and, supposedly, in so doing avoid a mass depletion of the faithful. Perhaps these requests center on certain questions of sexual morality: premarital sexual relations, birth control, AIDS prevention, and whether or not Catholics who have divorced and remarried should receive Communion. We think his definition is worth discussing further.

Isn't the gap between some of the Church's rules and the way Catholics live today just too big at the moment?

I need to take a few steps back to answer that. The ethical path, which forms part of the human being, is pre-religious. No person, be they a believer, an agnostic, or an atheist, can avoid the demands of what is ethical, which range from the most general principles—the most basic of all: "Do good and avoid evil"—to the most specific. As a man gradually discovers these principles and puts them into practice, he bridges the gap. I would say it's a gap in belief. There is also a gap between the Church and a counterculture, the sort of "Do as you please, it all ends up the same, we'll see each other in hell" attitude to which the tango "Cambalache" refers. And this attitude is equally common among agnostics, atheists, and believers. It's a question of living a double life, if you like. Or employing a double morality.

For example?

Let's see . . . I consider myself a Catholic, but I don't pay taxes. Or I'm unfaithful to my spouse. Or I don't pay enough attention to my children. Or I've got my father or mother tucked away in an old-folks home like a raincoat in a closet during the summer, complete with mothballs, and I never visit them. Or I swindle: I "fix" my scales or the meter in my taxi so they read in my favor. Basically, I live with fraud, defrauding not only the state and my family, but myself, too. Generally, when people talk about a double life they think of a person who has two families or a priest with a girlfriend. But everything that makes our way of living and the ethics that form part of our being fraudulent constitutes a double life. Ultimately, the challenge of living an ethical life, like

the challenge of living a religious life, consists of
behaving in accordance with these principles.

We agree that, with regard to certain issues, there is
widespread social acceptance . . .

I would say that there is a devaluation of the exercise
of ethical principles in order to justify a lack of
compliance with them. For example, and I'm
drawing on a typical example here, when I'm
chatting with people I often ask them whether they
pay their taxes, because it's a question that should be
asked, and many people reply in the negative. One of
the arguments they put forward is that the state
steals this money from them. "I put that money aside
and give it to the poor instead of it ending up in
some bank account in Switzerland," they tell me. In
this way, they soothe their consciences easily. Few
people think of conducting a deal entirely honestly
nowadays. There's almost always an element of
deceit involved in selling someone the Brooklyn

Bridge, and this is accepted because "everybody does it." We often say, "That's no longer the case" or "Times have changed." All these expressions are a kind of excuse for our failure to comply with ethical principles based on other people's poor behavior.

But certain perceptions and behaviors do change with the passage of time, and not always for the worse . . .

The fact is that, in general, cultures are progressing in terms of the appeal of a moral conscience. It's not what's moral that's changing. What's moral doesn't change. We carry it inside us. Ethical behavior is part of our being. What happens is that we are continuously defining it more clearly. For example, there is now an increasing awareness of the immorality of the death penalty. It used to be maintained that the Catholic Church supported it, or at least didn't condemn it. The latest version of the catechism asks that it be abolished. In other words,

the Church has become more aware of the fact that
life is sacred and that not even a terrible crime can
justify the death penalty. The same could be said
with regard to slavery, which is not to say that it's not
still occurring in different forms.

In what way is that the case?

We currently have hidden forms of slavery that are
just as cruel as the earlier ones. Today nobody would
even think about loading a cargo of slaves onto a
plane, never mind the fact that they'd be sent to
prison. But we know that there are Bolivians who go
to Argentina and work in exploitative, inhuman
conditions or in illegal workshops and who end up
in the slums around the capital and greater Buenos
Aires. We know that there are Dominican women
brought into the country to work as prostitutes.
These are all forms of modern slavery. In any case,
I am sure that just as the moral conscience of
different cultures progresses, people also refine
conscience to the extent to which they want to live a

better life, and this desire is not just religious but human.

But doesn't the Church ask too much with regard to certain aspects of human behavior, like those relating to sexual morality?

The Church preaches what it believes is best for people, what will make them most complete, happiest. But a degrading reductionism often occurs. Let me explain: the most important thing about a sermon is the message of Jesus Christ, which in theology is known as the *kerygma*. It summarizes the core Christian tenets: that God is in Jesus, He made Himself man in order to save us, He lived in the world like one of us, He suffered, He died, He was buried, and He came back to life. This is the *kerygma*, the message of Christ, which causes astonishment and leads to contemplation and belief. Some people believe straightaway, such as Mary Magdalene. Others believe after a period of doubt. And others need to put their finger in the wound, like Thomas.

Each individual has his own way of coming to believe. Faith is the encounter with Jesus Christ.

Are you saying, then, that some people are more preoccupied with sexual issues than with the core elements of the religious message?

That's my point exactly. After communing with Jesus Christ comes reflection, which is the role of the catechism. Reflection on God, Christ, and the Church, from which the Church's principles, the moral and religious rules, which do not contradict the human ones, but rather endow them with a greater degree of completeness, are deduced. Generally, I observe a degradation of the religious message in certain enlightened Christian elites due to a lack of living the faith.

Can you give an example of where you see this?

I see it in the fact that these people don't pay attention to the *kerygma* but instead move straight to the catechism, preferably the section on morality. It's enough to listen to some sermons, which ought to be kerygmatic, with an element of the catechism, but which turn out to be moral, or catechistic. And within that morality, although less so in sermons than on other occasions, people prefer to talk about sexual morality, about anything that has some link to sex. The fact that you're allowed to do this but you're not allowed to do that. The idea that someone is to blame and that someone else isn't to blame. In doing this, we relegate the treasure of the living Christ, the treasure of the Holy Spirit in our hearts, the treasure of living a Christian life, which has so many other implications beyond the questions of a sexual nature, to being of secondary importance. We overlook an extremely rich catechism, with the mysteries of faith and the creed, and end up focusing on whether or not to march against the passing of a law that would allow the use of condoms.

It seems that those topics motivate some of the faithful more than the prospect of going out to spread the word of the Gospel . . .

With regard to the so-called law on reproductive health, some groups of a certain leaning within the enlightened elite wanted to go to schools to recruit students to protest against the law because they believed that it was primarily a law against love. Of course, culturally love has become sexualized, to the point that in many cases it comes down to buying and selling, of mere consumerism. But the archbishopric of Buenos Aires was against the children taking part, arguing that that's not what children are for. To me, a child is more sacred than a legislative development. I forbade them from recruiting anyone under the age of eighteen. I allowed them to seek out those who could vote. This obviously reduced the pool of young people in school, because the majority of children graduate at seventeen. In any case, some groups turned up with students from two schools in greater Buenos

Aires. Why was there this obsession with bringing children to the protest? Those children saw things they had never seen before: aggressive transvestites and feminists singing violent protest songs. So the grown-ups took the children to see some very unpleasant things.

Surely they needed to boost their numbers.

But you shouldn't resort to minors for that. Children should not be used. Let me tell you an anecdote. A seminarian with extreme ideological beliefs is ordained as a priest. In a few days he has to give First Communion to the girls attending a school run by nuns. What a lovely thing it will be to talk to them about the beauty of Jesus! But no: before the Communion he remembers the conditions for receiving it: fasting for an hour, being in a state of grace, and . . . not using birth control! They were all just little girls in white dresses, and he berates them on the subject of contraception. That's the kind of distortion this can lead to. That's what I mean when

I talk about the descent from the beauty of the
kerygma to sexual morality.

**One very controversial issue is the Church's refusal
to allow those who have been divorced and who have
remarried to receive Communion. What would you
say to people in that situation who are suffering as a
result of being unable to receive the Eucharist?**

That they get involved in the parish community; that
there are things in the parish they can do. They
should try to be part of the spiritual community,
which is what the pontifical documents and the
Church's magisterium advise. The pope indicated
that the Church would stand by them. Being
unable to receive Communion is obviously painful
for some. In those cases, it's important to explain the
issues carefully. There are some cases where this
turns out to be difficult. It's a theological
explanation that some priests explain well and
people understand.

Let's talk about the battle against abortion.

I consider that to be part of the battle in favor of life from the moment of conception until a dignified, natural death. This includes care of the mother during pregnancy, the existence of laws to protect the mother postpartum, and the need to ensure that children receive enough food, as well as providing health care throughout the whole length of a life, taking good care of our grandparents, and not resorting to euthanasia. Nor should we perpetrate a kind of killing through insufficient food or a nonexistent or deficient education, which are ways of depriving a person of a full life. If there is a conception for us to respect, there is a life for us to care for.

Many say that opposition to abortion is a religious issue.

Well . . . a pregnant woman isn't carrying a toothbrush in her stomach, or a tumor. Science has taught us that from the moment of conception, the new being has its entire genetic code. It's impressive. Therefore, it's not a religious issue but, rather, a clear moral issue with a scientific basis, because we are in the presence of a human being.

Is the moral status of the woman who has an abortion the same as that of the person who performs it?

I wouldn't speak in terms of moral status. But I do feel much greater . . . not sadness but, rather, compassion, in the biblical sense of the word—by which I mean pity and empathy—for a woman who has an abortion under who knows what pressure, than I feel for the professionals—or the nonprofessionals—who do this for money and with a singular coldness.

Furthermore, the clinics that perform illegal abortions "get rid" of the women immediately, out of fear of possible arrest and the police turning up.

They send them packing, and if they hemorrhage, "that's their problem." This coldness contrasts with the crises of conscience, the remorse that many women who have abortions experience a few years later. You have to sit in a confessional and listen to these outpourings, because they know they killed a child.

Doesn't the Church block a lot of the paths that would avoid a great many abortions by opposing the distribution of contraception and, in some places, limiting sex education?

The Church is not opposed to sex education. Personally, I believe that it ought to be available throughout children's upbringing, adapted to different age groups. In truth, the Church always provided sex education, although I acknowledge that it hasn't always been adequate. What happens is that nowadays a lot of the people who wave banners in support of sex education see it as separate from a human person. Therefore, instead of getting a law in favor of sex education for a complete person, for love, they end up with a law in favor of sexual activity. That is our objection. We don't want the human being to be degraded. That's all.

CHAPTER 9

The Chiaroscuro of
Conscience

We could not conclude our conversation about the
Church without talking about the incidents of sexual abuse of minors committed by priests, and the future of
celibacy.

The numerous scandals involving pedophile priests that
erupted primarily in the United States led the Holy See to
adopt an extremely strict stance with respect to these serious
situations, meant to eliminate any and all suspicion of a
cover-up. But these scandals also stirred up the debate on
celibacy, given a supposed relationship between the two, a
debate that usually included, although in a weaker argument,
the problem of the growing shortage of priests.

Therefore, we thought it relevant to raise three key questions: Would the elimination of celibacy reduce the incidence of sexual abuse? Would it foster growth in the number of priests? Might this become an option in the near future?

The cardinal did not take long to respond.

Let's see . . . I'll begin with the last question: whether or not the Church is ever going to change its position with regard to celibacy. First, let me say I don't like to play mind-reader. But assuming that the Church did change its position, I don't believe it would be because of a lack of priests. Nor do I think celibacy would be a requirement for all who wanted to embrace priesthood. If it did, hypothetically, do so, it would be for cultural reasons, as is the case in the East, where married men can be ordained. There, at a particular time and in that particular culture, it was so, and it continues to be so today. I can't stress enough that if the Church were to change its position at some point, it would be to confront a cultural problem in a particular place; it would not be a global issue or an issue of personal choice. That is my belief.

But should it not confront it at some point?

Right now I stand by Benedict XVI, who said that celibacy should be maintained. Now, what kind of effect will this have on the number of those called to the priesthood? I am not convinced that eliminating celibacy would cause such an increase in those called to the priesthood as to make up for the shortage. Indeed, I once heard a priest say that eliminating celibacy would allow him to not be alone and to have a wife, but with that he would also be getting a mother-in-law. [Laughter.]

Let's suppose it would have other advantages . . .

Joking aside, it has many advantages.

But what do you say to those who think it could prevent incidents of sexual abuse?

Seventy percent of cases involving pedophiles happen within the family or the neighborhood environment. We have read stories of boys abused by their fathers, grandfathers, uncles, and stepfathers. In other words, they are psychological perversions that existed prior to choosing a life of celibacy. If there is a priest who is a pedophile, this perversion existed within him before he was ordained, and celibacy does not cure that perversion. They either have it or they don't. Therefore, we must be very careful who we admit into the priesthood. In the seminary in Buenos Aires, we admit roughly forty percent of those who apply. We monitor their progress very carefully. There are many who do not have the calling, and they leave, and down the line they marry and end up being wonderful laypeople in the parish.

Was it always so strict, or has it become more so since the wave of scandals?

The requirements became stricter long ago. Everyone must take a thorough exam, and that determines the selection. A person with a psychosis of any kind could be prone to narcissism, dishonesty, or criminal behavior. I remember the case of a boy who was acting very strangely. I arranged for him to see a psychiatrist, one of the top five interpreters of the Rorschach test in Argentina. The psychiatrist determined he was in the presence of one of the worst cases of paranoid psychosis he had ever seen. But the selection has to be rigorous not only on the human level but the spiritual level as well. We have to insist on a life of serious prayer—I always ask the seminarians how they pray—and a deep devotion to God and to others.

Notwithstanding the monitoring in seminaries, there continue to be those who abandon the priesthood, primarily to get married.

Celibacy is a choice in life, as is living in poverty, for example. There are times a priest can come to doubt himself, if he meets a woman in the parish and thinks he's fallen in love. Priests are faced with situations of, shall we say, falling in love, and that's normal. It is a cross to bear, and a new chance to reaffirm the choice in God. But one must be careful to differentiate between true love and mere excitement or sexual attraction. There are times when a priest does fall in love and must reassess his vocation and his life. Then he must go to the bishop and tell him, "I've made up my mind . . . I didn't know I was going to feel something so beautiful . . . I truly love this woman," and he asks to leave the priesthood.

And what do you do in these cases?

I am the first to share in this moment of a priest's life; I stay with him; I accompany him on his spiritual journey. If he is sure of his decision, I even help find him work. What I don't allow is a double life. If he can't lead his ministry, I ask that he stay home. We request what is called "dispensation," permission from Rome, and then he would be allowed to receive the sacrament of marriage. He must not scandalize the Church or harm the souls of the parishioners. God has mercy for all.

But there are psychologists who say that the Church plays on one's guilty conscience, and priests, in turn, who warn of the loss of the meaning of sin.

For me, feeling you have sinned is one of the most beautiful things that can happen to a person, if you take it to its ultimate end. Let me explain: Saint Augustine, speaking of redemption, and seeing the sin of Adam and Eve and the passion and resurrection of Jesus, said, "Good is the sin that made us worthy of such redemption. This is what we sing on Easter night: 'Good guilt, good sin.'" When someone realizes he is a sinner and is saved by Jesus, he admits that truth to himself and discovers the hidden pearl, the buried treasure. He discovers how great life is; that there is someone who loves him so deeply that He gave His life for him.

So then, in your opinion, the loss of the meaning of sin makes finding God more difficult?

There are some who feel righteous, who in some way accept the catechism, the Christian faith, but do not have the experience of having been saved. It is one thing for someone to tell you about a boy who was drowning in the river and someone diving in to save him; it is another to see it, and yet another if it's me who is drowning and someone dives in to save me. There are those who have been told this but did not see it, didn't want to see it, or didn't want to know what happened to that boy, who always had ways of avoiding the sense of drowning and, therefore, the experience of knowing what it is. I believe that only the greatest sinners have that grace. I often say that the only glory we have, as Saint Paul says, is that of being sinners.

In the end, it winds up an advantage for the believer. [Laughter.]

Well, let's not forget that the nonbeliever can also benefit from his shortcomings. If an agnostic or an atheist knows he has behaved badly, feels sorry about it, and wants to overcome the situation, he then becomes a better person because of it. In that way, that shortcoming acts as a springboard for his growth. The mayor of a large European city once said that every night he ended his day by examining his conscience. Although he was agnostic, he knew his life had meaning, and he made an effort to correct his behavior. His mistakes helped him become a better person.

That view at least allows one to consider the issue of guilt in the Catholic Church in another way.

Definitely. That's why, for me, sin is not a stain I need to clean. What I must do is ask for forgiveness and reconcile myself to it, not go to the dry cleaner around the corner. I need to go and find Jesus, who gave His life for me. This is an idea that is quite different from sin. In other words: sin properly assumed is the privileged place of personally finding Jesus Christ our Savior, of rediscovering the deep meaning that He has for me. In short, it is the possibility to live the wonder of having been saved.

To conclude this topic, let's turn to a quote from John Paul II, who observed a paradoxical situation: a growing indifference toward religion on the one hand, and a strong search for religion on the other, not always through orthodox ways.

Exactly. There is a denial of God due to secularization, the selfish egoism of humanity. And there are a thousand ways to search for God that require one to be careful not to fall into a consumer experience or, at its extreme, a kind of "immanent transcendence," that still does not result in true piety. What happens is that it is more difficult to enter into personal contact with God, a God that waits for me and loves me. The pantheism in the air, like a spray, does not last. At the end of this kind of search we need some kind of idol, and we end up adoring a tree or seeing God on a tree.

It is also true that many people say they believe in God, but not in priests.

And that's just fine. Many priests are not worthy of their belief.

CHAPTER 10

A Country
Struggling to Take Off

I n a country like Argentina, which goes from crisis to crisis, it is imperative that we reflect on the reasons it has been unable to reach its potential and provide its people with all the benefits it has. We wanted to share an article with Bergoglio by a former president of Uruguay, Julio María Sanguinetti, in which he states, "Someone once said that countries could be classified into four categories: first, the developed countries; next, the underdeveloped countries; third, Japan, whose development cannot be explained; and finally, Argentina, whose underdevelopment cannot be explained." Apart from the irony, it is an astute observation, a provocative assertion, that raises many questions.

In light of that observation, we asked Cardinal Bergoglio three related questions:

Could there be a disadvantage to having such
potential wealth? To what extent were Argentines
harmed by having, in some way, everything given to
them, unlike the reality that the immigrants left
behind? Was it necessary for the country to live
through a crisis like the one at the beginning of this
century, in order to become aware of the cruel
paradox that, in a country that has the capability
to feed three hundred million people, malnutrition
still exists?

First, I would like to make a couple of relevant
points. According to the Italians, you throw a seed
in the street in Argentina and a plant springs up.
And cows do not conceive out at pasture but rather
in stables. In my father's day, in his mountain
house in northern Italy, the stable was built right up
against the house so that the heat from the animals
would act as heating. The animals did not go out to

pasture: the grass and grain were brought to them.
The truth is that I don't know if our great wealth has
contributed to making things easy for us, but I can
say that we have not exploited what we have. On
God's judgment day, we will count ourselves among
those who ignored the gifts we were given and who
did not use them productively, not only in terms of
agriculture and raising cattle but in mining as well.
The mineral wealth of Argentina is impressive; we
have many mountains, of course. And despite our
long coastline, we are not a fish-eating culture, nor
do we fish for export. In other words, throughout
our history, we have not created jobs tied to our
natural resources. It cannot be that most jobs in
Argentina are found around the large cities such as
Buenos Aires or Rosario. It just can't be.

But it is . . .

Surely you know the story about the ambassadors
who go to see God to complain because, unlike their
countries, Argentina had been endowed with such

riches, and the Almighty responded, "Yes, but I also gave them Argentines." Kidding aside, clearly we have not been up to the task. But there is still time to change our ways.

The growth in the number of those living in poverty is significant. In Argentina, the percentage of those living in poverty rose from 4 percent in the early seventies to more than 50 percent during the crisis in 2001. Today there are so many people going hungry.

On the occasion of the festival of San Cayetano— Saint Cajetan—the patron saint of bread and work, I cited the words of a song by Father Julián Zini, who points out that it is impossible to starve to death in the blessed land of bread, because it is a great injustice that in our blessed country, in which, as I said, God gave us everything, there is not enough food or enough jobs. It is a great injustice and flagrant lack of responsibility in distributing our resources. When the Church mentions this, it is immediately criticized for attacking the government. Aside from a few brief periods, when things seemed to look up, the number of people living in poverty has continued to increase. It is not a new problem.

Is it a problem of mistaken economic policies or something more complicated?

I would say that, deep down, it is a problem of sin. For four years Argentina has been living a sinful existence because it has not taken responsibility for those who have no food or work. It is everyone's responsibility: it is mine, just as it is the bishops', all Christians', and those who spend money without any clear social conscience. Here in Buenos Aires, in the upscale area of Puerto Madero, there are thirty-six restaurants that are not inexpensive. At one end is the Villa Rodrigo Bueno, and at the other the well-known 31 Retiro house. In both there are people going hungry. This shows a lack of social conscience. On the rare occasion that someone gives to the poor,

he does so not even looking the person in the eye, so
as to avoid feeling guilty.

That's a strong statement.

As I mentioned in a visit to the radio station at the
shrine of San Cayetano, it is our duty to share our
food, clothing, health, and education with our
brothers. Some may say, "This priest is a
communist!" That's not it. What I am saying is pure
Gospel, and be careful, because we are going to
be judged by this. When Jesus comes to judge us, He
will say to some, "Because I was hungry and you
gave me to eat, I was thirsty and you gave me to
drink, I was naked and you clothed me, I was sick
and you visited me." And they will ask the Lord,
"When did I do that? I don't remember." And He
will respond, "Every time you helped the poor you
helped me." But He will also say to others, "Go
away, because I was hungry and you gave me
nothing to eat." And He will also condemn us for
the sin of blaming the government for poverty,

when it is a responsibility we must all assume to the extent we can.

The problem is that there are large segments of the younger generations that do not have even the most basic education and who did not grow up in a culture of work. The social mobility that characterized Argentina, that of "my son, the doctor," is, at the very least, in jeopardy.

That may be, but there is much we can do to turn that around. Take the example of the work of Father José María Di Paola in the Barracas district of Buenos Aires. Padre Pepe, as he was known, offered drug addicts an alternative: a school for arts and trade, an idea which was first tried during a previous crisis in Europe. With the Argentine crisis of 2001, it was revived because the situation was the same. After two years, kids came out with degrees, recognized by the state as specialized workers. They are trained as they go. The good thing about work, going back to what I was saying before, is that one sees the result and feels "divine," like God, able to create. In a certain sense, one feels the way a man and a woman do when they are holding their firstborn in their arms. The ability to create changes their lives. The kid who works feels the same way. The culture of work, combined with healthy pastimes, is irreplaceable.

Will a crisis as severe as the one early this century make us reflect on our situation?

Allow me to prove my point using the case of Japan that Julio María Sanguinetti mentioned. At the end of the Second World War, Japan was devastated. Not only did it endure the horrifying destruction of entire cities, which left its mark on the entire painful aftermath of the war, it also suffered a great cultural failure that was set forth in the emperor's radio message when he said that he was not divine. It was at that point that the Japanese began to rebuild their country. In their bombed-out ports, boys and men threw themselves into the sea with wrenches, retrieving pieces of iron from sunken boats and airplanes that had been shot down, in order to use these for foundations. This would pave the way for the Japanese steelworks. They were starting from scratch.

And do you think that Argentina could have reacted in the same way?

What I can say is that there are many examples throughout history that demonstrate the creative capacity to generate work, and coming out ahead seems to occur, especially in the worst of crisis, when there is nothing left to do. Maybe Argentina is at that point.

CHAPTER 11

Building a Culture of Cooperation

Another common explanation of Argentina's decline is the inability of its citizens to act together as a society. The potential of individuals is not expressed collectively. Cardinal Bergoglio points out that the country is suffering from something else, something worse than not knowing how to put a team together: a long-standing climate of dissension that works against the quest for consensus and the formation of a national plan. In contrast, Bergoglio stresses the need for a "culture of cooperation."

Can you tell us what you are proposing?

Of course. A culture of cooperation is the only way
for families and towns to move forward. There is a
frieze on the cathedral in Buenos Aires that depicts
Joseph with his brothers. One might ask what Joseph
and his brothers have to do with the main church in
Buenos Aires. This frieze was made during the time
of the National Reorganization, as a symbol of the
Argentines' desire to come together. Of course that
is still to come, because it is hard for us Argentines
to agree. We are especially narrow-minded, quick to
go off and do our own thing. An example of this is
the roughly nineteen hundred candidates who were
registered in the 2007 elections in the province of
Misiones! In the presidential election that year
there were eighteen candidates. So we are either a
fantastic nation with eighteen geniuses who can
lead the country, or we are a nation of fools who
can't agree. Again, mutual agreement is very
difficult for us. We have a tendency to point out the

things that divide us and not what unites us, a
tendency that fuels conflict, not agreement. I would
go as far as to say that we like fighting among
ourselves.

Is there some historical explanation for this?

Maybe *caudillismo,* the system of military
dictatorship, had a lot to do with it. We must
remember that the National Reorganization was
brought about by *caudillos* who came together but
failed to accomplish anything. When Carlos Menem
was president and wanted to repatriate the remains
of a *caudillo* like Juan Manuel de Rosas, he was faced
with great opposition. When he finally did it, instead
of it being a national event—the laying to rest in his
country of the remains of a man who, for better or
worse, gave his life fighting for his country—the
nationalists took it and turned it into a partisan act.
Out came the characteristic red ponchos. Even the
priest who read the prayer for the dead put it on

over his cassock, even more tactless, because the
priesthood should be accepting of all. Without
doubt it was a new display of our national
dissension.

We suppose that in a time of crisis, when
everything we take for granted becomes uncertain,
the way we look at things becomes even more
important.

The word "crisis" is related to words meaning
"sieve." The sieve saves what needs to be saved and
gets rid of the rest. Right now I believe we must
devote ourselves to a culture of cooperation or we
are lost. The totalitarian approaches of the last
century—fascism, Nazism, communism, and
liberalism—lead to fragmentation. They are
collective approaches masked as unification,
principles without organization. The most human of
challenges is organization. For example, unbridled
capitalism fragments economic and social life, while

the challenge of a society is the opposite: establishing ties of solidarity.

How do we move toward a culture of cooperation?

For the time being, by reflecting on what exactly the culture of human cooperation is, a culture that has, at its foundation, the idea that the other person has much to give me, that I have to be open to that person and listen, without judgment, without thinking that because his ideas are different from mine, or because he is an atheist, he can't offer me anything. That is not so. Everyone has something to offer, and everyone can receive something. Prejudging someone is like putting up a wall, which then prevents us from coming together. Argentines are very judgmental. We immediately label people so that, deep down, we can avoid the encounter and the dialogue. And so we wind up fostering dissension, which, in my opinion, reaches the level of social pathology.

Is it just a question of prejudgment, or is there
something else?

I believe it is also a problem of communication
fostered by three actions: spreading misinformation,
defamation, and slander. The first lies in not giving
the complete information about a person or an
incident and quickly engaging in gossip. For me,
spreading misinformation is the most dangerous of
the three, because telling part of the truth confuses
and misleads people. Defamation and slander are
more serious morally than spreading incomplete
information, but may not be as harmful. On the
other hand, our way of thinking leads us to
indulge in gossip. What is gossip? It is a truth
taken out of context. It's like the tango that says,
"Shame on you, neighbor, for wearing white after
you have sinned." And the psychology of gossip
leads to dissension. A bishop once called me,
angered by something someone had said that had
been based on gossip, or a partial truth. I suggested

that he pay no attention and to regard it as
neighborhood gossip.

*Psychologists warn that when one lacks identity he
looks for affirmation through negative behavior, by
discrediting other people.*

Exactly. One does not say "I am," but rather "I am
not." We put other people down in order to raise
ourselves up. We can agree that lack of identity is a
lack of belonging. At this point I feel it is important
to distinguish among nation, country, and *patria*, or
homeland. Country is the geographic environment,
which has a geopolitical location. Nation is the
national organization, with its history and laws, and
patria is our heritage, the most precious thing we
have, what we have received from those who came
before us. All that our predecessors did for our
patria, the nation, and the country forms a legacy
that must not just be handed down but
strengthened. This is what differs from the

restorationists, for whom *patria* is something that is
passed down and maintained just as it was received.
In that way, in my opinion, *patria* is killed, it is not
allowed to grow. All patrimony should be utopian;
its roots must be maintained, but it should be passed
on to those who have the desire to see it continue to
develop. Let's not forget that utopias lead to growth.
Of course, the danger is not just in falling into the
trap of reflecting on the past, of patriotic duty, in
being satisfied with what one has received and not
looking any further, but also in the nonhistorical
utopia, the one without tradition, the pure fantasy.

**With that in mind, how can one assert that identity
will lead to cooperation?**

In my opinion, there are three elements that
strengthen the identities of a person and a country.
First, there is transcendence, which looks toward
God and makes transcendence possible for others.
And for the nonbeliever? He can transcend, at least
through others, and therefore not be isolated. But

without believing, I do not have transcendence. Second, there is diversity, an organized and harmonious diversity that enriches a nation. And, finally, there is vision, where instead of looking back, there is a focus on the future, on where we want to and must go. These are three elements that strengthen a person and a country, and that can be defined by what they say no to. They say no to atheism and the lack of transcendence, no to the supremacy of the powerful who generate a narrow-minded hegemony, which flattens diversity, and no to progress that is not rooted in history. In this way, cooperation can be achieved.

Do you think you are doing everything you can to contribute to a culture of cooperation? Were you not accused by some of being a leader of the opposition to Néstor Kirchner's administration?

I am saddened by any kind of dissension. I admit that I am guilty, on more than one occasion, of not having used all the means at my disposal to resolve a conflict with someone. That also saddens me, and I regard it as a sin. But to consider me the opposition seems misleading. I believe the people applaud my efforts, or rather the efforts of the Church, to build bridges between people.

After you and other Church officials met with Kirchner in 2003 when he became president, you never met with him again. Should we infer from what you say that you did not request another meeting because conditions were not favorable?

I don't want to look back. I will just reiterate that my intent and the intent of the Church is to build bridges between people, but with dignity.

So if Kirchner had asked to meet with you, you would have agreed?

Of course. In fact, in 2006, I sent him a letter inviting him to a memorial service honoring the five priests and Pallottine seminarians who were murdered during the dictatorship, on the thirtieth anniversary of the massacre that took place in San Patricio Church.

I never knew you had invited him.

I even asked him to preside over the ceremony when he arrived at the church, as it was not a Mass; throughout his term of office I always treated him with the proper respect due to him as the president of our country.

Did you continue to meet with other members of that administration?

Of course, just as with everyone else. When leaders from different realms request my guidance, my answer is always the same: Talk to each other, talk, talk, talk.

CHAPTER 12

"I Also Like Tango"

Cardinal Bergoglio was always extremely punctual when welcoming us to his chambers. Only once was he late in coming out to meet us. We assumed that some matter of urgency had held him back.

While we waited in the reception, we spotted him walking by with a thermos and some bills. This struck us as odd, since time is not usually set aside for parishioners between appointments. A few minutes later, we saw him bidding farewell to a married couple of humble origins and their two children. We later found out that the thermos (filled with hot water to make *mate*) and the money were for the family, who were from the Chaco region and who had met the cardinal by chance and wished to pay their respects before heading back home to their province. Despite the unexpected nature of the visit, Bergoglio greeted them with open arms, took an interest in their situation, and sent them on their way with a warm embrace.

"Apologies for the delay, but the family's visit was not in my plans," he apologized, as we made our way to the visitors' room.

What the cardinal had no way of knowing was that the endearing episode we had just witnessed made us change the approach of our chat. We decided to set the standard list of questions on a particular topic aside and, instead, delve further into his personality. For once, the questions on religious, social, and cultural issues fell off the agenda. We wanted to hear about his day-to-day life, his habits, his tastes, his feelings. We wanted to reveal the man behind the high-ranking ecclesiastic dignitary.

Bergoglio accepted our proposal on one condition: "One thing straight, nothing in the style of Corín Tellado," he said, referring to the Spanish author of romance fiction. "A little wouldn't hurt," we countered, our curiosity piqued. So we began.

How would you introduce yourself to a group of
people who have no idea who you are?

I am Jorge Bergoglio, priest. I like being a priest.

A place in the world?

Buenos Aires.

A person.

My grandmother.

How do you like to keep up on current affairs?

Reading the newspapers. I switch on the radio to
listen to classical music.

Internet?

I might follow the example set by one of my
predecessors, Cardinal Juan Carlos Aramburu, who

started using it once he had retired, after turning
seventy-five.

***You travel on the subway a lot. Is that your
preferred mode of transport?***

I almost always use it, because it is the fastest, but I
prefer the bus, so I can see the street.

Ever had a girlfriend?

Yes. She was part of a gang of friends we'd go out
dancing with.

What brought the relationship to an end?

I discovered my religious calling.

***Do you have any family members who also embraced
their religious vocation?***

Yes, my sister Marta's son. He's a Jesuit priest
like me.

Any hobbies?

As a young man I collected stamps. These days, reading, which I greatly enjoy, and listening to music.

A literary work?

I love the poetry of Friedrich Hölderlin. Also, many works of Italian literature.

Such as?

I must have read Alessandro Manzoni's *I Promessi Sposi* (*The Betrothed*) four times. The same is true of *The Divine Comedy*. I find Dostoyevsky and Joseph Maréchal moving.

Borges? You knew him.

That goes without saying. Moreover, Borges had a genius's knack for talking on any subject without bragging. He was a very wise man. The image I

retain of Borges and his attitude toward life is that
of a man who puts things in order, ordering books
on the shelves like the librarian he was.

Borges was agnostic.

An agnostic who said the Our Father every night
because he had made a promise to his mother, and
who died in the presence of a priest.

A musical composition?

Among those I most admire is Beethoven's Leonore
Overture No. 3, in the version by Wilhelm
Furtwängler, who, as I see it, is the finest conductor
of certain of Beethoven's symphonies and the works
of Wagner.

Do you enjoy tango?

Very much so. It's something that comes from
within. I consider myself quite knowledgeable on the

two ages of tango. From the first age, my favorites
are Juan D'Arienzo's orchestra and, as far as singers
go, Carlos Gardel, Julio Sosa, and Ada Falcón, who
went on to become a nun. I read the last rites to
Azucena Maizani. I knew her, as we were neighbors,
and when I found out that she'd been taken to the
hospital, I paid her a visit. I remember running
into Virginia Luque and Hugo del Carril. From
the second age, I'm a great admirer of Ástor
Piazzolla and Amelita Baltar, who is the finest
singer of his work.

Can you dance the tango?

Yes. I danced it as a young man, although I preferred
the *milonga*.

A painting?

White Crucifixion by Marc Chagall.

What kind of movies do you like?

The films of Tita Merello, naturally, and the Italian Neorealist movies, which my parents introduced me and my siblings to. They wouldn't let us miss a single movie with Anna Magnani or Aldo Fabrizi, which, as with the operas, they would explain to us. They'd give us two or three basic notions to get us started; then we'd head off to the neighborhood cinema, where they'd show three movies in a row.

Any movie you recall in particular?

Babette's Feast, most recently, really moved me. And many Argentine films. I remember the Legrand sisters, Mirtha and Silvia, in the movie *Claro de Luna*. I was eight or nine. A great Argentine movie was *Los Isleros*, directed by Lucas Demare, a masterpiece. And a few years ago I enjoyed *Esperando la Carroza* (*Waiting for the Hearse*), but I no longer go to the movies.

Your favorite sport?

I played basketball as a young man, but I liked going to the stadium to watch soccer. The entire family would go, including my mother (who accompanied us until 1946), to see San Lorenzo, the team of our hearts. My parents were from Almagro, the club's neighborhood.

Any special soccer memory?

The team's outstanding season that year. There was a goal by René Pontoni almost worthy of a Nobel Prize. It was a different era. The worst thing you could call the referee was good-for-nothing, shameless, a sellout . . . In other words, a world away from today's epithets.

What languages do you speak?

I can chat a bit in Italian [in reality, we can confirm that he speaks it perfectly]. As for other languages,

I ought to specify that, because of a lack of practice, these are languages I "used to speak." I had a smattering of French, and I could get by in German. The hardest one for me has always been English— above all, the pronunciation, because I don't have an ear for it. And, of course, I understand Piedmontese, the sound of my childhood.

What was your first trip abroad?

Colombia, in 1970. Later I visited all of the novitiates in Latin America. In Mexico I came across a gated community for the first time, something that didn't exist in Argentina back then. I was astonished to see how a group of people could cut themselves off from society.

When did you first make it to Europe?

On September 4, 1970. I went to Madrid first, before visiting the novitiates in the rest of Europe. Among

other trips that followed was one to Ireland to
practice my English. I remember traveling at
Christmas in 1980; I was seated beside an elderly
Jewish couple on their way to Jerusalem. A delightful
pair. When it was announced after dinner that
ice cream would be served to mark the occasion,
the man muttered sadly that he couldn't eat it, as
they had already had meat. As you know, they
cannot mix meat and milk. But seconds later
he looked at me with a sly grin and proclaimed:
"But today is Christmas, Father!" And he ordered
himself a serving, just like that. I could have
kissed him . . .

**What was it like to meet up with your family in
Italy? How did it feel to visit the region of your
ancestors?**

What can I say? I felt completely at home speaking
in Piedmontese. I met one of my grandfather's
brothers, my uncles, my cousins. My oldest cousin is

seventy-eight, and when I visit her it's as if I had always lived there. I give her a hand with the housework, I set the table . . . In any case, I try to avoid traveling.

Why's that?

Because I'm a homebody. I love my home. I love Buenos Aires.

How did you see Argentina from abroad?

With plenty of nostalgia. After a while, I always wanted to come back. I remember that when I was in Frankfurt, working on my thesis, I'd take a stroll in the evenings to the cemetery. You could see the airport from there. One time I bumped into a friend who asked what I was doing, and I replied, "Waving to the planes. I'm waving to the planes bound for Argentina."

*What represents a great sacrifice for you in your
daily life?*

> Many things. For example, staying up past midnight
> to pray.

*On that subject, how many hours do you sleep
a day?*

> It depends, but it tends to be around five. I go
> to bed early and wake up at four in the morning
> without an alarm clock. I do, however, take a
> forty-minute siesta.

What to you is the greatest of all virtues?

> Well, the virtue of love, of giving oneself to another,
> and doing that from a position of gentleness. I find
> gentleness so attractive! I always ask that God grant
> me a docile heart.

And the worst of all sins?

If I consider love to be the greatest virtue of all, it should logically follow that hatred is the worst of all sins, but what I find most repellant is pride, or arrogance, feeling that one has "made it." Whenever I've caught myself feeling like I have "made it," I've felt great inner shame and begged for God's forgiveness, for no one is free from such things.

What is the first thing you would save from a burning house?

My breviary and my agenda. I would be truly sorry to lose them. My agenda contains all of my appointments, addresses, telephone numbers. And I'm very attached to my breviary; it's the first thing I open in the morning and the last thing I close before going to bed. When I travel I sometimes have to take the two volumes of the breviary, and I carry them on. Inside, between the pages, I keep my

grandmother's creed and the poem by Nino Costa
that I recited earlier.

**Do you remember any letters from your
grandmother?**

There is one that has a special place in my heart, one
she wrote half in Italian and half in Spanish, back in
1967, on the occasion of my ordination. Just in case
she passed away beforehand, she took the precaution
of writing it out early so that, together with a present
she had also planned, they could be delivered to me
on the day I became a priest. Fortunately, she was
still alive when I was ordained and she was able to
give me both things. I have that letter here. [He
takes out the breviary and leafs through its pages.]

Would you read it to us?

Of course. "On this beautiful day on which you hold
Christ our Savior in your consecrated hands and on

which a wide path leading to a deeply held vocation opens up before you, I bequeath to you this humble gift of little material, but great spiritual, value."

And what does her creed say? [He searches his breviary once again.]

In one paragraph she wrote: "May these, my grandchildren, to whom I gave the best my heart has to offer, lead long and happy lives, but if one day hardship, illness, or the loss of a loved one should fill them with grief, may they remember that one sigh directed to the tabernacle, home to the greatest and most august martyr, and a glance toward Mary at the foot of the cross, may cause a soothing drop to fall on the deepest and most painful of wounds."

What was it like when, as just another priest at the Jesuit residence in Córdoba, you found out you were to become auxiliary bishop, of your beloved Buenos Aires, no less?

The man who was apostolic nuncio at that time, Monsignor Ubaldo Calabresi, used to call me to sound me out about certain priests who were no doubt candidates to become bishop. One day he called me and told me he thought our conversation should be face-to-face this time. Since the airline flew Buenos Aires–Córdoba–Mendoza, he suggested that we meet in the Córdoba airport while the plane was traveling to and from Mendoza. And so we spoke there; it was May 13, 1992. He asked me a range of questions on serious matters, and when the plane, which had touched down from Mendoza and was set to take off on its way back to Buenos Aires, was boarding, he told me, "Ah . . . one last thing . . . you've been named auxiliary bishop of Buenos Aires, and the appointment will be made official on the twentieth." He came out with it just like that.

And how did you take the news?

My mind went blank. As I said before, my mind
always goes blank after a shock, good or bad. And
my initial reaction is also always wrong.

Was your reaction the same when you were named
coadjutor bishop, with the right to succeed Cardinal
Quarracino?

The same. Since I was his general vicar, when
Quarracino requested a coadjutor from Rome, I in
turn asked him not to send me to any diocese, but
rather to name me an auxiliary bishop again, in
charge of a regional vicarage in Buenos Aires. "I'm a
native of the city and I wouldn't know what to do
with myself outside Buenos Aires," I explained. But
at mid-morning on May 27, 1997, Calabresi called
and asked me to lunch with him. We were drinking
coffee, and I was all set to thank him for the meal
and take my leave when I noticed that a cake and a
bottle of champagne had been brought in. I thought

it must be his birthday, and I was just about to offer my best wishes. But the surprise came when I asked him about it. "No, it's not my birthday," he replied, grinning broadly. "It so happens that you are the new coadjutor bishop of Buenos Aires."

Since we're on the subject, how did it feel to hear your name repeated over and over again in the Sistine Chapel during the counting of the votes for the successor to John Paul II?

[Bergoglio became serious and looked somewhat tense. Finally, he broke out into a smile and replied:] At the beginning of the conclave the cardinals swear an oath to secrecy; we cannot talk about what happens there.

At least tell us how it felt to see your name among the leading candidates to become pope . . .

Shame, embarrassment. I thought that the journalists had taken leave of their senses.

Or had a little inside information.

They covered all the bases with their predictions. They said, just in case, that there were nine potential popes and picked out two Europeans, Ratzinger included, and two Latin Americans, among others. That way, they reduced their margin for error and boosted their chances of getting it right.

So, we journalists have very active imaginations . . .

Very active.

.   .   .

The surroundings in which Bergoglio lives and works also speak volumes about his personality. What first struck us was that he does not use the office intended for the arch-bishop, a spacious room on the second floor, which, while sober, could give off an aura of power, even superiority. As far as we were able to tell, he used it as a storage space. His office is housed on the same floor, but in a very small room, smaller still than the office of his secretary, who does not even keep his schedule. He jots down his appointments in a notebook himself. His small desk is perfectly ordered. Dotting the wall under the window are some prayer cards, snapshots of his pastoral activity, and a very moving image of a malnourished aboriginal native of the north.

One floor up is his bedroom, the same one he occupied as a general vicar. Austere in the extreme, it has a simple wooden bed, a crucifix from his grandparents Rosa and Juan, and an electric heater (although the building has central heating, he does not turn it on unless his whole staff is there). Other than that, his quarters are very tidy. "A woman drops by on Tuesdays to clean," he told us. It was quite clear that he makes his bed himself every day. Just opposite, separated by a corridor (home to a pedestal displaying a stunning image of a seated Christ, the Christ of patience, the virtue he holds so dear), is his personal chapel, similarly threadbare.

Finally, in an adjacent room, he has a library filled with books and papers. Bergoglio commented that he is organizing his papers so as not to "leave any work behind when I die." He confessed that he is getting rid of much of his writing. "I want to leave as little as possible behind me when I take my leave from this world," he explained. But he admitted to holding on tight to one document. It is a scrap of paper, faded by the passing years, with a heartfelt declaration of faith, which he wrote "at a time of great spiritual intensity," shortly before being ordained, and which today he would happily write again.

It reads:

I wish to believe in God the Father, who loves me as a son, and in Jesus, our Lord, who fills me with the Holy Spirit in my life so that I may smile and thus carry me to the kingdom of eternal life.

I believe in my history, which was infused with the loving gaze of God, who, on a spring day of September 21, crossed my path and invited me to follow Him.

I believe in my pain, though often made barren by my selfishness, in which I seek refuge.

I believe in the abjection of my soul, which seeks to swallow whole without giving back . . . without giving back.

I believe in the kindness of others, and that I must love them without fear, without ever betraying them in search of my safety.

I believe in the religious life.

I believe I wish to love in abundance.

I believe in everyday death, which burns, and from which I flee, but which smiles at me, inviting me to accept it.

I believe in the embracing patience of God, as gentle as a summer evening.

I believe that my father is in heaven at the Lord's side.

I believe that Father Duarte* is also there, interceding on behalf of my priesthood.

I believe in Mary, my mother, who loves me and who will never leave my side.

And I await the surprise of each day in which love, strength, betrayal, and sin shall become manifest, which

---

* Father Duarte heard his confession that September 21.

shall accompany me until that final meeting with that
magnificent face, of which I know nothing, from which
I constantly flee, but which I wish to know and
love. Amen.

A handful of portraits of loved ones round out his personal library. For example, a photo of a young engineering student, who died in an accident, and a painting by his Jewish friend Daniela Pisarev, the painter he married to a Catholic. Our gaze caught on a vase brimming with white roses on one of the shelves in his library, with an image of Saint Thérèse of Lisieux behind it. "Whenever I have a problem," he told us, "I ask the saint not to resolve it, but to take it in her hands and help me accept it, and, as a sign, I almost always receive a white rose."

.   .   .

As we were taking our leave, Bergoglio introduced us to an Alitalia pilot, Aldo Cagnoli, who had dropped by to pay his respects. They had made each other's acquaintance on a Rome–Buenos Aires flight and formed a great friendship.

Cagnoli, who had a degree in sociology, had brought him a copy of his doctoral thesis on airline terrorism, which he had dedicated to the cardinal. As he was planning to publish a book on the subject, he had also come to request that Bergoglio write the prologue.

We thought that he might be able to shed new light on Bergoglio, and, on a separate trip of his to Buenos Aires, we asked him to discuss his friendship with the cardinal.

At our meeting, Cagnoli mentioned that he had met Bergoglio on April 20, 2005, on a flight between Rome and Buenos Aires, and that he had reached out because he was curious, moved by a newspaper article he had come across about an Argentine cardinal of Italian origin who went about his pastoral duties with a firm moral conviction and great humility.

Ever since then, Cagnoli had wanted to go beyond the brief and partial information in the article. "When I met him for the first time on the plane and we exchanged a few opinions, he was just as I had always pictured him, right down to some of his quirks," he admitted. "I was struck," he went on, "by his great ability to make the person he was speaking to

feel at ease and on the same wavelength, his severe appear-
ance in contrast to his warmth and, above all, his extraordinarily unaffected manner."

At the end of their first encounter, during which the
two men discovered that they had both been born on
December 17, Bergoglio invited Cagnoli to visit him in Buenos Aires. Cagnoli jumped at the first chance he got, even
though his time in the Argentine capital was short. Their
friendship grew over the course of successive meetings in
Buenos Aires and Rome, with lengthy discussions on an
array of topics, covering everything from cuisine to ethical
and social issues. They even shared some time at the home of
the pilot's parents. Cagnoli was struck by Bergoglio's ability
to find topics of conversation and reflection, beyond the
seemingly naive and involuntary provocations of the pilot's
father, a craftsman with deep-seated communist convictions.

"During one visit, for example, my father told him how
hard he found it to sculpt the image of Christ on the cross he
had promised him as a gift," Cagnoli recounted. "His problem, as a craftsman, lay in imagining Jesus as a man suffering, deeply angered by what was happening to him. 'I never
thought of it like that,' Bergoglio replied, 'but perhaps Christ,

in his humanity, was in some way angered by his dreadful suffering.'" Some time later, from Buenos Aires, Cagnoli's father sent Bergoglio a beautiful image of Christ with a resigned, tender expression on his face. "My father was deeply moved by that reply," Cagnoli remarked.

Cagnoli admires Bergoglio's ability to find the good in everyone and to see everything from different angles, while keeping to a well-defined path. "The greatness of the man, in my humble opinion," he summed up, "lies not in building walls or seeking refuge behind his wisdom and office, but rather in dealing with everyone judiciously, respectfully, and with humility, being willing to learn at any moment of life; that is what Father Bergoglio means to me."

He finished by saying: "His greatness lies in his down-to-earth nature combined with his tremendous wisdom, his open mind combined with his moral rectitude, the ability to listen to and learn from everyone, even when he has so much to teach us. I believe that he does simply, and at the same time extraordinarily, what so many men both inside and outside the Church ought to do and, regrettably, fail to do."

CHAPTER 13

The Difficult Path
Toward a Nation
of Brothers

I f there is one homily that is repeated in the documents of
the Argentine bishops of the last few decades, it is the
one referring to national reconciliation following the political violence that plunged the country into mourning until
the return to democracy in 1983. Military coups, terrorist
attacks by groups at both extremes of the ideological spec-
trum, and an atrocious policy of repression originating from
the very heart of the state during the last military dictatorship left deep wounds. Wounds that continue to damage the
consciousness of the Argentine people and that raise serious
questions about those responsible, many of whom remain
protected by impunity. Wounds that continue to be a source

of sorrow for the relatives of the victims, thousands of parents who have nowhere to go to mourn for their children, because they are still "disappeared." Wounds that have scarred those who suffered illegal detention, torture, and lengthy exiles forever.

The role of the Church during those years, and, in particular, during the so-called National Reorganization Process led by successive military juntas, sparked controversy, since accusations of weakness—and even complicity on the part of certain members of the clergy—in the face of systematic violations of human rights have never been in short supply.

In this context, the concept of national reconciliation—based on truth, justice, and forgiveness—brandished by the bishops aroused mixed interpretations. There were those who believed it was a front for an offensive to avoid too much scrutiny of the past and to bring an end to the judicial review (therefore suggesting support for any law on the cessation of legal action that might come into force), thus, importantly, guaranteeing impunity to the soldiers who were involved. In contrast, others saw this sermon as a contribution to the peace process, in particular during the moments when the newly reinstated democracy was laboriously taking its first steps.

So how should the sermon in favor of reconciliation be interpreted? What are the real meaning and scope of Christian forgiveness? How does it complement judicial punishment? Should forgiveness be granted to someone who doesn't repent? Does it imply some form of atonement on the part of the forgiven as a matter of course? In short, is it realistic to think that a reconciled country is possible, or is a reconciled country just a utopia and must it be left to time to heal the wounds? Finally, did the Church rise to the occasion sufficiently during the military dictatorship to become, over the course of the years, a credible voice for national reconciliation?

We believed it was essential to broach this subject.

The Gospel states that you have to love your enemy—
Bible scholars clarify that this should be interpreted
as "wishing him well"—and to forgive seventy times
seven times. Aren't these rather utopian premises
that, in some way, are contrary to human nature?

Jesus is tremendous on this point: He doesn't weaken, and He leads by example. When He was

treated so badly—a false conviction, the worst
kind of torture, and those responsible washed their
hands of the situation—He exclaimed, "Father,
forgive them, they know not what they do." He
managed to find an excuse and so was able to forgive
them. With regard to the sentence "If your enemy is
hungry, feed him; if he is thirsty, give him something
to drink," there has recently been a very good
translation into Spanish. Until now, we used to read:
"For in so doing you will heap coals of fire on his
head." The idea of heaping coals of fire on someone's
head didn't sound quite right to me. The new
translation changes it to: "For in this way his face
will burn with shame." This, in some way, indicates a
strategy: arriving at such a human response, one that
is such a credit to us—being ashamed of something
bad we've done. Someone with no sense of shame
has lost the final safeguard that limits the extent
of his awful behavior; he's rotten to the core. Jesus
is very clear on this. Note! He doesn't say, "Forget
about it."

People often say, "I forgive, but I don't forget."

I can't forget the things people have done to me,
but I can look at them through different eyes, even
though I may have suffered. We mature with the
passing of the years; as Juan Perón would say, we
"recoup," we become wiser and more patient. And
when the wound has more or less healed, we gain
distance. This is an attitude that God asks of us:
forgiveness from the heart. It means I don't hold
what you did to me against you; it has been
transformed to create part of the balance of losses
and gains. Perhaps I'm not going to forget about it,
but I'm not going to hold it against you. Or, rather,
I'm not going to harbor a grudge.

*So it's not a case of wiping the slate clean and
starting afresh, but really only of starting afresh.*

There's no clean slate. Once again, it's not possible
to forget. In any case, I calm my heart and ask God

to forgive the person who wronged me. Note: It's
very difficult to forgive without reference to God,
because people have the capacity to forgive only
if they have the personal experience of being
forgiven. And, generally, we have this experience
with God. Of course, sometimes, forgiveness can be
granted humanly. But only someone who has had to
ask forgiveness at least once is capable of granting
forgiveness. For me there are three words that define
people and constitute a compendium of attitudes—
incidentally, I don't know whether I can claim to
have them myself—and they are: permission, thanks,
and forgiveness. The person who doesn't think to
ask permission barges through life, going ahead with
his own agenda without bothering about other
people, as if other people didn't exist. In contrast,
the person who asks for permission is more humble,
more open, more conciliatory.

What can be said of a person who never says
"Thanks" or who feels in his heart that he has
nothing for which he should be grateful to anybody?

There is that very eloquent Spanish saying, "Manners make the man." Gratitude is a flower that blossoms in noble souls. And, finally, there are people who think it unnecessary to ask forgiveness for anything. They suffer the worst sin: the sin of pride. And let me say it again, only someone who has had to ask forgiveness and who has experienced forgiveness can forgive. For this reason, anyone who doesn't ask for forgiveness is lacking something in his day-to-day life. Either he was not given a chance to learn properly or he has been taught badly by life.

But is it possible to forgive someone who doesn't show remorse for the wrong he's committed? And who, in the words of the catechism, shows no willingness to somehow atone for the wrong he's done?

In the homily for a Corpus Christi Mass, I said something that scandalized some people, perhaps because they thought I was making some kind of apology for all the bad things that had happened to us and trivially calling for people to start a new chapter. It was when I referred to people who curse the past and don't forgive; more than that, I mentioned those who use the past to gain revenge. Basically, I asserted that we have to bless the past with remorse, forgiveness, and atonement. And forgiveness has to go hand in hand with the other two concepts. If someone wrongs me, I have to forgive him, but that forgiveness is received by the other person only when he shows remorse and atones. You can't say, "I forgive you, and so nothing happened here." What would have happened at the Nuremberg trials if they had adopted this attitude toward the Nazi leaders? Many of them atoned via execution; for others, it was prison. Don't misunderstand me, I'm not in favor of the death penalty, but it was the law at the time and it was the atonement that society demanded in accordance with the prevailing law.

So forgiveness isn't a one-way act, dependent solely on the will of the person who forgives.

I have to be prepared to grant forgiveness, and it becomes effective only when the person to whom it is granted is ready to receive it. And they can receive it when they feel remorse and want to atone for what they did. Otherwise—to use a soccer term—the forgiven person remains offsides. Granting someone forgiveness is one thing; having the capacity to receive it is quite another.

If I hit my mother and then ask her to forgive me while I know that I'd beat her again if she did something else I didn't like, she might grant me forgiveness, but I won't receive it, because my heart will be closed. In other words, in order to receive forgiveness, you have to be ready for it. This is why that famous expression of "weeping for one's sins" appears in the accounts of great conversions in the stories of the saints, to describe an act so Christian as weeping for the sins that have been committed, which implies remorse and the intent to atone for them.

But when the offenses are extremely serious, when
terrible crimes are committed, isn't a mechanism of
denial, and, to a certain extent, justification,
triggered by the argument "I had no other choice
but to commit them"?

I think this is true with the smallest offenses, not
just with the biggest ones. I've experienced—and
I've discussed this with my confessor—moments of
intense internal enlightenment when I realized the
extent of the failings in my life and the sins for
which I hadn't atoned. I observed my actions with
different eyes, and I was terrified. If I felt panic in
these instances of bright light between one period
of darkness and another, when I became aware of
the social consequences of what I'd done, or stopped
doing, I can easily imagine that there are people
who, when faced with massive mistakes, employ a
mechanism of denial or all kinds of arguments so as
not to die of distress.

At any rate, the problem in Argentina is that "it was nobody . . ."

In this context, it's important to acknowledge the protagonists of the turbulent events of the first few decades of our national history, who owned up when they killed one another. For example, "I shot this man." Signed "Lavalle." During the political violence that took place during the latter part of the twentieth century, almost nobody admitted responsibility for anything, and if anyone did, they didn't always give any indication of remorse or an intention to atone for what they'd done. During the last military dictatorship—whose human rights violations, as we bishops said, are made much more serious by the fact that they were committed by the state—things got so bad that thousands of people were "disappeared." If the wrong isn't acknowledged, isn't that an extreme, hideous form of not taking responsibility?

Some people have attitudes of revenge. Do you think
that the role of, for example, Hebe de Bonafini, the
president of the Mothers of the Plaza de Mayo, is
helpful in the search for reconciliation?

We have to put ourselves in the place of a mother
whose children were kidnapped and who never
heard any more about them. They were flesh of her
flesh; she didn't even know how long they were
imprisoned, how many sessions of torture with
electric shocks and violent beatings they suffered, or
how they were killed. I imagine these women
searching desperately for their children and coming
up against the cynicism of the authorities, who
humiliated them and sent them from pillar to post.
How can we not understand what they're feeling?

Was the Church a staunch defender of human rights
during those years?

In order to answer this question, we have to keep in
mind that, like wider society, the Church—which

consists of all baptized Catholics—came to realize what was happening gradually. Nobody was fully aware of what was happening at the start. In my own case, I must admit that I started out with a lot of limitations when it came to interpreting certain events: when Juan Perón returned to the country in 1973 and the Ezeiza massacre took place, I didn't understand what was going on at all. Nor when Héctor Cámpora resigned the presidency. At that point, I didn't have enough political information to understand all that.

However, we were becoming increasingly aware of the guerrillas, of their intention to gain a foothold in Tucumán, and of the terrorist attacks, which involved civilian victims who had nothing to do with politics and young people carrying out their military service. Then President Isabel Martínez de Perón issued her decree (which ordered "the annihilation of subversive activity"). At that point, we began to realize that things were serious. At the same time, it seemed like the whole world began "knocking on the barracks doors." Almost everyone, including the

vast majority of political parties, supported the 1976
coup. If I'm not mistaken, the only ones who didn't
were the Revolutionary Communist Party, although
it's also true that nobody, or very few people, had
any idea what would follow. We have to be realistic
about this; nobody should wash their hands of it. I
hope that the political parties and other
organizations will ask forgiveness like the Church
did (the bishops undertook an examination of
conscience in 1996 and, in 2000, carried out a mea
culpa as part of the Jubilee).

***There are those who maintain that the Church was
well aware of what was happening during the
dictatorship.***

I reiterate that at the beginning, little or nothing
was known; we became aware gradually. I myself,
as a priest, knew that something serious was
happening and that there were a lot of prisoners, but
I realized it was more than that only later on. Society
as a whole recently became fully aware of events

during the trial of the military commanders.
Of course, certain bishops realized the kinds of
methods that were being used on the prisoners
before others did. It's true that there were some
more perceptive pastors who took great risks.
Monsignor Vicente Zazpe, the archbishop of Santa
Fe, was one of the first to realize the sort of thing
the dictatorship was doing following the kidnapping
and savage torture of Adán Noé Campagnolo, who,
until the coup, had been mayor of the provincial
capital.

There were others, too, such as Miguel
Hesayne, Jorge Novak, and Jaime de Nevares, who
immediately began to take strong stances in defense
of human rights. There were others who did a lot
but spoke out less. And, finally, there were a few
who were naive or lazy. On the other hand,
sometimes, subconsciously, an individual doesn't
want to see things that could become unpleasant,
doesn't want to accept that they're really true. It
happens with parents whose child is a drug addict or
a gambler or has some other vice. It's a very human

response. I truly found it difficult to see until they started to bring people to me and I had to hide the first one.

We'll talk more about that later. It's often said that the bishops favored discreet efforts over public declarations out of fear that the latter would cause an increase in the rate of executions. Was this a formal strategy? Didn't the Church end up a silent accomplice?

It's true that the Church did, in part, follow this strategy. However, in spite of the discreet nature of the Church's efforts, the bishops' declarations left no room for doubt. And anyone can read them, because they were compiled in a book, which we unveiled on the twenty-fifth anniversary of the publication of our document *The Church and the National Community.* The third chapter, "The Church and Human Rights," contains the main ones. And contrary to the suggestions of certain ill-intentioned journalists, they're complete, with no omissions. The Church spoke out. Furthermore, there's a pastoral letter dated May 15, 1976, which reflects the concerns the bishops were already experiencing, and another from April 1977, which warns about torture. There were also others dating from Isabel Perón's presidency. In any case, some of the thoughts expressed are doubtful in tone because, as I said, the Church really didn't know what was happening. But events like the massacre of the Pallottine priests and seminarians gave increasing force to their statements.

Whenever the Church spoke out in the following years about the need to achieve reconciliation, there was never any shortage of people who believed they saw an endorsement of impunity behind its message. What do you think?

Absolutely not. I want to make myself clear: justice must run its course. It's true that after great global

upheavals, after massive wars, the sociopolitical
mechanism of amnesty always comes into play. After
the Second World War, amnesties were granted in
various countries, but there were also trials for those
responsible. France had to deal with Pétain and his
collaborationists, and it acted generously. While
de Gaulle was harsh, he was afraid of treating them
unjustly, since, at the time, it was very difficult to
judge whether or not it would be a good thing for
France to collaborate with the Nazis. They didn't kill
Pétain, but sent him to French Guiana. De Gaulle
wanted to remove all thirty-five bishops with links
to Pétain from office. Then Angelo Roncalli (later
Pope John XXIII), the apostolic nuncio in Paris,
arrived on the scene and three or four of them
ended up retiring. I think a distinction was made
between ambiguous situations, the result of fear,
and criminal situations. While the former are
understandable, the latter are not. Pétain acted as
he did in the belief that it was the patriotic thing to
do. But he was mistaken, even though his intentions
were good. If that had not been the case, he would

have swung for it, because the French don't beat
around the bush.

Such topics often draw comparison with the case of
John Paul II, who forgave the man who tried to
assassinate him, but justice still ran its course.

Of course. Mehmet Ali Ağca's trial still took place.
The pope forgave him, but he was still found guilty
and remained in jail until he served his term, when
he was deported to Turkey, where he was jailed again
for crimes he had committed in his own country.
This case clearly demonstrates what I was saying
before with regard to an individual being able to
grant forgiveness from the heart, but there also being
a need for remorse and atonement on the part of the
other person. In the version of events I know, which
I believe to be true, when the pope went to visit him
in jail, at no point did Ali Ağca show any sign of
remorse. On the contrary, he said to the pope,
"I don't understand why you didn't die . . . my
trigger never fails."

In any case, doesn't the search for true reconciliation imply that something must be given up? Doesn't it demand magnanimous gestures?

We always have to give things up. Something has to be given up for a state of reconciliation to be reached. Everyone has to do it. But it's important to be careful that it's not something that affects the essence of justice. Perhaps the person who must grant forgiveness is asked to give up their resentment. Resentment is bitterness. And living with bitterness is like drinking urine, like eating your own feces; it suggests that you don't want to leave the pigsty.

Pain, on the other hand, is a different kind of sore, an open field. Resentment is like a house where squatters live piled one atop another with no view of the sky. While pain is also like a house where there are a lot of people living on top of one another, but you can still see the sky. In other words, pain is open to prayer, to affection, to the company of a friend, to a thousand things that give an individual dignity.

Pain is a healthier condition. That's what experience has taught me.

The mother of Michelle Bachelet, the president of Chile, has said that she once met her torturer in an elevator, that she forgave him and experienced a great sense of peace.

Forgiving someone always does good—it is part of what you were asking me about in your previous question: the virtue of magnanimity. A magnanimous person is always happy. A pusillanimous person, with a crumpled heart, never achieves happiness.

Is forgiveness the thing that makes men and women most like God?

Love is what brings us closest to God. Forgiveness makes us resemble Him by virtue of being an act of love.

CHAPTER 14

The Darkness That Engulfed Argentina

As Pope John Paul II's life ebbed away, speculation about the candidates likely to succeed him grew, and the name Bergoglio held a prominent place in nearly all the forecasts of the specialized press. Around that time, a newspaper accusation published a few years earlier in Buenos Aires, about the cardinal's supposedly compromising role during Argentina's military dictatorship, was once again bandied about. Indeed, on the eve of the conclave that was to elect the successor of the Polish pontiff, a copy of an article containing the accusation was e-mailed to the voting cardinals with the aim of jeopardizing the Argentine cardinal's chances.

The article alleged that the cardinal was partly responsible for the 1976 kidnapping of two Jesuit priests who were working in a shantytown in the city's Flores district, two months after the coup d'état. According to this version, Bergoglio—who at the time was the provincial superior of the Company of Jesus in Argentina—asked Father Orlando Yorio and Father Francisco Jalics to give up their pastoral work in the slum district and, as they refused to do so, informed the military that the priests were no longer under the Church's protection, thereby leaving the way clear for their kidnapping, and thus putting their lives at risk.

The cardinal never spoke out in response to the accusation, nor did he ever refer to other accusations from the same source regarding alleged connections with members of the military junta (nor, in general, did he publicly discuss his stance during the dictatorship). Considering the goal of our interviews, however, he acknowledged that the subject could not be avoided and agreed to give his version of the facts and of the role he took on during the period of darkness that engulfed Argentina. "If I said nothing at the time, it was so as not to dance to anyone's tune, not because I had anything to hide," he stated.

Your Eminence, you let slip earlier that during the dictatorship you hid people who were being persecuted. How did you do that? How many did you protect?

I hid some people at the Jesuit Colegio Máximo in San Miguel, in greater Buenos Aires, where I lived. I don't remember exactly how many, but a few. After the death of Monsignor Enrique Angelelli—the bishop of La Rioja who was known for his commitment to the poor—I sheltered three seminarians, theology students, from his diocese, in the Colegio Máximo. They weren't hidden, but they were looked after, protected.

In the small bus on his way to La Rioja to take part in a tribute to Angelelli on the thirtieth anniversary of his death, the bishop of Bariloche, Fernando Maletti, met one of those three priests, who is now living in Villa Eloisa, in the province of Santa Fe. Maletti didn't know who he was, but when they got talking, the priest told him that when he and the other two priests were at the Colegio

Máximo they used to see people coming to do long,
twenty-day retreats, and that after a while they
realized the so-called retreats were a screen for
hiding people. Maletti told me this later and said he
hadn't known anything about it, and that we ought
to spread the news.

Apart from hiding people, did you do anything else?

I once smuggled a young man out of the country via
Foz do Iguaçu in Brazil. He looked quite a bit like
me, carried my identity card, was wearing priest's
clothing, with the clerical collar, and in that way
I managed to save his life. I did what I could for my
age and, with the few contacts I had, to plead for
people who had been kidnapped. I got to meet with
General Jorge Videla and Admiral Emilio Massera
twice. In one of my attempts to talk to Videla,
I managed to find out which military chaplain
celebrated the Mass and persuaded him to say he
was sick and to send me in his place. I remember

that I celebrated Mass in the residence of the
commander in chief of the army, before the whole
Videla family, one Saturday afternoon. Afterward,
I asked Videla if I could have a word with him, with
the intention of finding out where the arrested
priests were being held. I didn't go to any detention
centers, except once, when I went to an air base near
San Miguel, in the neighboring district of José C.
Paz, to try to ascertain what had happened to a
young boy.

Is there any case that you particularly remember?

I remember meeting one woman who was brought
to me by Esther Balestrino de Careaga, who, as
I mentioned earlier, was my boss at the laboratory
and who taught me so much about politics; she was
later kidnapped and murdered, and is now buried in
the city's church of Santa Cruz. The woman who
came to see me, from Avellaneda, in greater Buenos
Aires, had two sons, who had been married only two

or three years. Both were communist militant worker delegates who had been kidnapped. She was a widow, and her sons were all she had left. How she cried! It was a scene I will never forget. I made some inquiries but got nowhere, and I often reproach myself for not having done more.

Was there any case that had a happy ending?

I recall the case of a young catechist who had been kidnapped and on whose behalf I was asked to intercede. In this case, too, I had little chance of success and very little influence. I don't know if my inquiries had anything to do with it, but the fact is, thank God, the boy was released shortly afterward. His family was overjoyed! That is why I say again: After something like that, how can one not understand the reaction of so many mothers who went through a terrible ordeal, but, unlike this case, never saw their children again?

What action did you take with regard to the kidnapping of the priests Father Yorio and Father Jalics?

To answer that, I must start by saying that they were planning to set up a religious congregation, and they gave the first draft of the Rules to Monsignors Eduardo Pironio, Vicente Zazpe, and Mario José Serra. I still have the copy they gave me. The superior general of the Jesuits, who then was Father Pedro Arrupe, told them they had to choose between the community they were living in and the Company of Jesus, and ordered them to move to a different community. As they persisted in their project and the group broke up, they asked to leave the Company. It was a long, internal process that lasted more than a year. It was not a hasty decision of mine. When Yorio's resignation was accepted, along with that of Father Luis Dourrón, who was working with them—Jalics's couldn't be accepted, as he had taken the solemn vow; only the pope could accede to the request—it was March 1976,

the nineteenth, to be exact, that is, five days before
the government of Isabel Perón was overthrown. In
view of the rumors of an imminent coup d'état, I
told them to be very careful. I remember I offered
them the chance to come and live in the Company's
provincial house, in the interests of their safety.

**Were they in danger simply because they were
working in a shantytown?**

Yes. They lived in the so-called Rivadavia quarter in
the Bajo Flores district. I had never believed they
were involved in "subversive activities," as their
persecutors maintained, and they truly weren't. But
because of their proximity to some priests in the
shantytowns, they were too exposed to the witch-
hunt paranoia. Since they stayed in that
neighborhood, Yorio and Jalics were kidnapped
when the area was combed. Dourrón escaped
because when the operation took place he was
cycling around town and, seeing all the commotion,
rode away down Varela Street.

Fortunately, they were released some time later, first of all, because they could not be accused of anything, and, second, because we wasted no time. The very night I learned they had been kidnapped, I set the ball rolling. When I said I had met with Videla twice and with Massera twice, it was because of the kidnapping of these priests.

According to the accusation, Yorio and Jalics thought that you, too, considered them subversive, at least a little, and that you harassed them somewhat because of their progressive ideas.

I will not kowtow to those who want to pin me down like that. I've just explained, in all sincerity, my views regarding the work of those priests and the role I assumed following their kidnapping. Jalics comes to see me whenever he's in Buenos Aires. Once we even celebrated Mass together. He comes to give courses with my permission. He had an opportunity once when the Holy See offered to accept his resignation, but he decided to continue in

the Company of Jesus. I repeat: I did not throw them
out of the congregation, nor did I want them to be
left unprotected.

*In addition, the accusation says that three years
later, when Jalics was living in Germany and
Argentina was still under the dictatorship, he asked
you to intercede for him with the Foreign Ministry
to get his passport renewed without his having to
come back to Argentina, but that although you saw
to the formalities, you in fact advised the civil
servants in the Ministry of Foreign Affairs and
Worship not to approve the application because of
the priest's subversive background . . .*

That is not quite accurate. It *is* true that Jalics—who
was born in Hungary but was an Argentine citizen
with an Argentine passport—wrote to me while
I was still the provincial superior to ask me to do
this for him because he had a justified fear of
coming to Argentina and being arrested again.
So I sent the authorities a written request—not

mentioning the real reason, but stating that the trip was very expensive—for him to be able to get it seen to at the embassy in Bonn. I delivered the letter by hand, and the civil servant to whom I gave it asked me what had caused Jalics to leave so suddenly. "He and his friend were accused of being guerrilla fighters, but they had nothing to do with any such thing," I answered. "Give me the letter, then, and you'll get the reply in due course," he said.

What happened after that?

They denied the request, of course. The author of the accusation against me went through the file of the secretary of worship, yet all he mentioned was that he found a scrap of paper on which that civil servant had noted that he had spoken to me and I had told him they were accused of being guerrilla fighters. In short, he had made a note of that part of the conversation but not the other part, where I said that the priests were not involved in anything like that. Also, the author of the accusation omits the

fact that I wrote the letter making the request; I was
the one sticking my neck out for Jalics.

*It was also mentioned that you were instrumental
in Admiral Massera's being awarded the honorary
doctorate by the Jesuit-founded Universidad del
Salvador.*

I believe it was a professorship, not a doctorate.
I was not the sponsor. I was invited to the event,
but I did not attend. And when I found out that a
group had politicized the university, I went to a Civil
Association meeting and asked them to leave,
despite the fact that the university no longer
belonged to the Company of Jesus and that I had no
authority other than that of being a priest. I say this
because I then became linked to that political group.
Anyway, if I respond to every accusation made,
I get drawn into the game. Not long ago I was in a
synagogue taking part in a ceremony. I prayed a lot
and, while praying, I heard a phrase from one of the
books of wisdom that had slipped my mind: "Lord,

may I bear mockery in silence." It gave me much peace and joy.

. . .

When the young Father Jorge Bergoglio knocked on her office door, Dr. Alicia Oliveira thought it would be a meeting like so many others she used to hold as a criminal law judge in the mid-1970s. It never occurred to her that she and the priest would get along so well that they would become firm friends, a friendship that would eventually make her a qualified witness of Bergoglio's actions during the military dictatorship. Oliveira has a long track record as a human rights activist, a role she embraced ever since she started as a criminal lawyer. After the military coup, this activism cost her the post of magistrate; she was among the first to be dismissed.

She signed hundreds of habeas corpus writs for illegal arrests and missing persons during the last dictatorship, worked as a lawyer, and formed the first steering committee of the Social and Legal Studies Center (CELS, or Centro de Estudios Sociales y Legales), one of the most emblematic NGOs fighting human rights violations.

With the return of democracy she held several posts, including that of member of the National Constitution Convention of 1994 (elected as a member of the list of the Frente Grande, or Broad Front, a center-left dissident Peronist group); ombudswoman of the city of Buenos Aires from 1998 to 2003; and then—under the presidency of Néstor Kirchner—Special Human Rights Representative for the Ministry of Foreign Affairs, a post she held for two years until her retirement.

"I remember that Bergoglio came to see me at the court about a problem having to do with a third party, sometime in 1974 or 1975. We got to talking, and there was an empathy between us that led to further conversations. In one of our chats we talked about the imminent threat of a coup. He was the provincial superior of the Jesuits and was probably a lot better informed than I was. In the press they were even shuffling the names of future ministers. The newspaper *La Razón* had published that José Alfredo Martínez de Hoz was going to be minister of the economy," recalls Oliveira, adding that "Bergoglio was very concerned because of what he sensed was going to happen and, as he knew about my human rights commitments, he feared for my life. He even suggested that

I go and live in the Colegio Máximo for a while. But I didn't accept his offer and answered with a silly witticism that was a most unfortunate turn of phrase in view of everything that would happen later: 'I'd rather be captured by the military than have to go and live with priests.'"

However, the magistrate did decide to take some precautions. She told the court clerk, Dr. Carmen Argibay, whom she trusted completely—and who was eventually made a minister of the nation's Supreme Court of Justice, at Kirchner's proposal—that she was thinking of leaving in Argibay's care the two children she had at that time, so that she could go into hiding, for fear of being put under military arrest. In the end she decided not to do that, nor was she taken prisoner. Argibay, however, was arrested the very day of the coup. Oliveira desperately tried to find out where she was being held, until the jail in Devoto informed her she was there, but neither she nor the prisoner herself ever knew why Argibay was imprisoned for several months.

After the fall of Isabel Perón's government, Oliveira and Bergoglio met more frequently. "In our talks I could see that his fears were growing, especially with regard to the Jesuit priests in the settlement," says Oliveira. "I think that

Bergoglio and I began to realize early on what the military were like. Their penchant for the friend/enemy logic, and their inability to discern between political, social, or religious activism and armed conflict . . . so very dangerous. And we were painfully aware of the risks being run by those who were going into the lower-class districts. And not only them, but also the people who lived there and who could catch it on the rebound."

She remembers that she begged a friend of hers, a girl who used to go and teach catechism at the settlement—and who was not an activist at all—not to go back there. "I warned her that the soldiers didn't understand, and that whenever they saw someone in the district who didn't live there, they assumed they were an international Marxist-Leninist terrorist." It took a lot to make the girl understand. Finally, she left, and years later acknowledged that the advice had saved her life. "But others who stayed were not so lucky, and that's why Bergoglio was so worried about the priests in the shantytown and wanted them out of there," she affirms.

Oliveira remembers that Father Jorge was not merely concerned about locating Yorio and Jalics and getting them released; he also endeavored to find out where many other detainees were being held, and to smuggle others out of the country, like that young man who resembled him and to whom he gave his identity card. "I used to go to the Saint Ignatius retreat house, and I recall that many of the meals served there were farewell dinners for people whom Father Jorge smuggled out of the country," Oliveira says.

Bergoglio also managed to hide one family's book collection that included works by Marxist authors. "One day Esther Balestrino de Careaga called him, asking him to come to her house to give a relative last rites, which surprised him because they weren't religious, but when he got there, she explained that the real reason was to ask him to take her daughter's books, as her daughter was being watched. The daughter was later kidnapped and, eventually, released—unlike what was to happen to her," Oliveira remembers.

With regard to the stance of the Universidad del Salvador during the last dictatorship, and Bergoglio's role there, Oliveira is adamant that what she saw while at that center of higher studies could in no way be considered collusion with the dictatorship; far from it. "I don't know what happened at the university, but many of us sought shelter there," she stresses. She shared the professorship of criminal law with Eugenio Zaffaroni (someone else who was dismissed by the dictatorship but who, being a professor at the University of Buenos Aires, also reached the Supreme Court, promoted by Kirchner). And in her classes she would speak freely. "When I used to explain the law of trial by ordeal (the terrible ordeals imposed in the Middle Ages to establish someone's guilt or innocence), the students would say it was horrendous, and then I would tell them what was going on in our country; Bergoglio used to say that the soldiers would be coming to pick me up with the Green Falcon," she recalls, mentioning a symbol of state terrorism.

With her co-professor, Oliveira experienced an episode that in her view clearly illustrates Bergoglio's position regarding the dictatorship. Toward the end of the military government, in the preelectoral stage, Zaffaroni learned that the jurist, Charles Moyer—former clerk of the Inter-American Court of Human Rights—wanted to visit the country to convince the candidates how important it was for Argentina to adhere to the Inter-American Human Rights Convention (agreement of San José de Costa Rica). Since at the time Moyer was working at the Organization of American States, headquartered in Washington, D.C., the secretary-general, the Argentine Alejandro Orfila, on learning of his intentions, threatened to dismiss him if Moyer traveled to Buenos Aires. "Orfila had a lot of vested interests in the dictatorship," Oliveira points out. So Zaffaroni asked her what they could do to get Moyer over to Argentina, albeit on false pretenses. Oliveira thinks back: "What did I do? I appealed to Father Jorge, of course, who told me not to worry. Shortly afterward he dropped by with a letter in which the university invited Moyer to come and give a talk on the procedures of the Inter-American Court of Human Rights . . . a dreadfully boring subject! Professors of international law were convened for the occasion. Bergoglio asked me not to go near the place. The *gringo* didn't know what to talk about. Later, we discreetly took him to see the candidates. It was pathetic: hardly anyone had heard about the San José de Costa Rica agreement. On his return, Moyer sent Bergoglio a letter thanking him. And Raúl Alfonsín, as soon as he took office, ratified the agreement."

Nevertheless, Oliveira—herself critical of the actions of

many bishops during the dictatorship—acknowledges that there will always be some doubt about whether the members of the clergy who personally took care of victims of the illegal oppression followed the best strategy in prioritizing discreet action over publicly denouncing the regime. Was it the best thing for the safety of the victims? Could a superior of a religious community "take it upon himself" and stick his neck out? "The truth is I don't know what would have been best, or how the different echelons of the Church work." But she believes that the legitimate doubts—arising, often, from the perspective that comes with the passage of time—concerning the path that was taken do not invalidate conduct such as Bergoglio's. They certainly don't leave room for unfounded accusations.

That is why Oliveira considers the act of e-mailing to the cardinals who were preparing to elect the successor to John Paul II the article denouncing Bergoglio's alleged collusion with the dictatorship a "trashy intelligence operation." Especially because—she affirms—the journalist who wrote it "had written another article a few years ago in which he said very different things, in which he told the truth."

She does, however, admit to feeling relieved when she learned that Bergoglio had not been elected pope in the 2005 conclave. "The truth is that if they had elected him, I would have had a sense of loss, as he is almost like a brother to me, and, besides, we Argentines need him."

CHAPTER 15

Trusting in the Future

The twentieth century kicked off full of optimism. Could anyone possibly have imagined the two world wars? Or the Armenian genocide? Or the Jewish Holocaust? Or the scale of Stalin's cruelty? The self-evident political, social, scientific, and technological progress has not sufficed to free vast numbers of the world's population from abject poverty or to overcome the scarcity of commodities such as freedom and social justice. In fact, the divide between rich and poor has widened even further. Man has performed great feats, but has also been responsible for disastrous events. Religions have been hard-pressed to contend with modern-day challenges, the threat of fundamentalism, and, at times, very virulent attacks. Argentina went from being one of the world's leading countries to one that is lagging behind. What is the outlook for the twenty-first century?

In our last conversation we did not want to goad our subject into the role of soothsayer. We wished to find out if he has any grounds for hopefulness and what his main expectations, but also his major concerns, are for the future. Is he one of those who think the olden days were better and that today's world is going from bad to worse? Or is he among those who think that mankind, taken in perspective, with all our ups and downs, is advancing irreversibly? Are we moving toward a more religious era, or will the transcendent irredeemably lose ground? What role should the Catholic Church play in building a better society? Is it utopian to think about Christian unity? What lies ahead for Argentina?

Let's take it bit by bit. For me, hope is in the human person, in what lies in his or her heart. I believe in man. I'm not saying man is good or bad, just that I believe in man, in the dignity and greatness of the person. Life poses moral questions and we put our principles into practice, or not . . . because

sometimes we get caught up in circumstances and
succumb to our weaknesses. The twentieth century
was fantastic in many ways, and dreadful in others.
But are we better off now or worse? If we look at
history, we can see it has ups and downs. Some
people are like corks: certain circumstances push
them under, but then they bob back up to the
surface; meaning they always bounce back. I think
this applies, in general, to human nature, to all
people and all societies.

Let's face it, it's not easy to believe in man after
what happened in the last century.

Well, in fact, history does seem to be somewhat
calamitous, a moral disaster, a chaos of holistic
possibilities. When you see the empires built at the
cost of so much bloodshed and the oppression of
entire peoples; when you see genocides like those of
Armenia and the Ukraine, and the Jews, as you
mentioned . . . If you look at our recent, and not-
so-recent, history, it's enough to make you hold your

head in your hands. Today, at Mass, we read the passage from Genesis about how God regretted having created man because of all the evil things he had done. That is a key to interpreting history. Of course, whoever wrote it was not narrating historical fact, but merely giving a theological interpretation of human malice. So what is the Word of God telling us? That there are times in history when the dignity of man becomes debased. However, later on it reappears.

Do you really think your argument is convincing enough for all the people who are fearful, not just because of all that happened in the past, but because of things that are happening today?

We mustn't fear adversity. This brings to mind the character Catita in Argentine movies, played by Niní Marshall. Whenever anyone told her of some misfortune, she would say: "Tell me about it, ma'am." One can always say, "Tell me about it, ma'am." There's always someone worse off. What is the difference between the cases of children stolen for the purpose of cutting them up and harvesting their organs and the sacrificing of children in other cultures? That borderline with evil, the possibility of man becoming a monster, has always been there. Of course, as we are experiencing it now, we feel it more. In spite of everything, though, history keeps moving on. Man still also continues behaving altruistically, writing beautiful things, making poetry, painting, inventing, and developing science. As I believe in the future from the human standpoint, so I trust to it even more from the Christian perspective, on the basis of the presence of Christ in our midst.

So does that mean you believe civilization is advancing?

To answer that, I must first explain that there are two kinds of "uncivilization." One is the result of the preexisting chaos on which science—and everything else—acts, orders, and transforms, leading to cultural, scientific, industrial, and other kinds of progress. However, man has the potential to create another chaos, a second form of "uncivilization," if his inventions get out of hand and he ends up controlled by them, if scientific discovery supersedes him and he is no longer the master of the creation but a slave of his very inventions—say, when he starts experimenting with genes and cloning and ends up, perhaps, materializing the myth of Frankenstein. Or when he uses atomic energy in warfare. Or when he eagerly embraces antihuman laws, believing them to be progressive. That second form of ignorance, as I say, is the one that leads to disaster and, eventually, to man's great defeats, which are responsible for mankind having, somehow, to start all over again.

The trouble is that, as the Church has been warning us, science advances rapidly, whereas ethical principles seem to be on the wane.

That is true. That's why ethical dialogue is so important, but it has to be ethics with goodness.

I confess that I am scared stiff of untalented intellectuals and ethicists devoid of goodness. Ethics is a flowering of human goodness. It is rooted in the person's, or the society's, capacity for good. Otherwise, it becomes an ethicism, a false ethic and, in short, the great hypocrisy of the double standard. The person who tries to appear ethical, deep down has no goodness. This can be projected onto international relations. Let us consider, for example, that the AIDS virus is decimating whole populations in Africa. The inhabitants of a part of that continent are sentenced to extermination amid a certain amount of inaction.

Are you concerned about the falling birth rate in the first world and the increasing numbers of people who are alone?

Of course I'm concerned. It's a form of social suicide. By 2022, Italy will not have enough revenue in its retirement coffers—that is, the country will not have the funds to pay its pensioners. At the end of

2007, France celebrated having reached the figure of
two children per woman. But Italy and Spain have
less than one per woman. That means physical
spaces and social realities will be replaced; it implies
that other cultures and perhaps another civilization
will emerge. This will not take the same form as the
barbarian invasions of the year 400 or so, but the
territory left by some will be occupied by others.
As a result of the migrations, Europe may undergo
changes in its culture. Although, actually, that's not a
new phenomenon. Let's not forget that the extensive
Christian communities that inhabited northern
Africa for several centuries no longer exist today.

*Apropos of that, how do you see the future of the
Catholic Church? Will the new century be a
religious one?*

The Church should be accompanying nations in
their development on all fronts: the existential, the
moral, and the human, with all its new potential. It
has to help them grow in humanity because, after all,

man is the object of God's Revelation, made in
God's image. As Christians we can neither repudiate
that concept nor negotiate it. In other respects,
I believe the new century will be a religious one.
However, we'll have to wait and see in what way.
I repeat, religiousness is sometimes accompanied by
a sort of vague theism that mixes the psychological
with the parapsychological, and not always by a true
and deep personal encounter with God, as we
Christians believe it should be.

**Do you think any progress will be made in the
reunification of the Christian denominations?**

I start by welcoming the steps taken so far, and that
are still being taken with the ecumenical movement.
Catholics and evangelicals feel we are becoming
closer, living in harmony with our differences. We
are looking for a reconciled diversity. To get straight
to the question: I do not think we can, at the
moment, consider uniformity, or complete unity, but
we can consider a reconciled diversity that implies

walking together, praying and working together, and together seeking unity in the truth.

And how do you see Argentina's future?

Our society has moral and cultural reserves. Fortunately, the more down-to-earth our people are, the more solidarity they show. It is true that, occasionally, disturbing things occur, such as, some time ago, a fire in a shantytown in Buenos Aires, caused by a fight that broke out—poor versus poor—which threatened the reserves of solidarity, but, even so, we haven't lost them yet. The challenge is to remain alert and to hang on to them. When politicians start seeking solutions via agreements, they are wrong not to base those agreements on the solid moral reserve of our people. Otherwise, they are merely a contract that can be broken whenever we feel like it. It's true that the nation is battered, immersed in a somewhat anarchistic situation, but we are still in time to do good things for our *patria* because, I insist, we do have reserves.

Why do you use the term patria?

I prefer to talk about *patria* rather than country or nation. Country is, after all, a geographical fact, and nation is a legal, constitutional fact. However, *patria* is what lends a person identity. Someone who loves the place where he or she lives is not called a countryman or a nationalist but a patriot. *Patria* is related to *padre* (father); it is, as I said before, the land that receives the tradition of our fathers, that carries it on, that takes it forward. Our *patria* is what we inherit from our fathers in the now, for the purpose of carrying it on. Which is why those who talk of a *patria* detached from heritage are just as wrong as those who reduce it to heritage alone and will not let it grow.

In short, you have a moderately optimistic view of the future of the country and the world . . .

That is what I feel. I could be wrong. We will not see it, our children will. Like the story of the two priests who are talking about a future Council, and one asks the other, "Will a new Council abolish compulsory celibacy?" The other replies, "It would seem so." And the first one says, "Oh, well, we won't see it, but our children will." All joking aside, one should not confuse optimism with hope. Optimism is a psychological attitude toward life. Hope goes further than that. It's the anchor you toss into the future and can pull on to reach what you wish to attain. It's making an effort in the right direction. Besides, hope is theological: God is involved. That is why I believe life will triumph.

Reflections on the Poem
Martín Fierro

In his Easter 2002 message to the educational communities in the city of Buenos Aires, Cardinal Jorge Bergoglio gave a series of reflections about his homeland based on the epic poem *Martín Fierro*, written in the late nineteenth century by the Argentine José Hernández; they illustrate Bergoglio's views on national affairs with singular acuity and ingenuity.

MARTÍN FIERRO, A "NATIONAL" POEM

"National identity" in a globalized world

It's funny. Just the title of the book, even before I open it, suggests to me thought-provoking reasons for reflecting on the core components of our identity as a Nation. *The Gaucho Martín Fierro*—that was the title of the first edition. What do gauchos have to do with us? If we lived in the countryside, working with animals, or at least in rural villages, more in touch with the earth, it would be easier to understand. In our large cities, in Buenos Aires itself, many people will remember the horses on the carousels, or the livestock pens in the Mataderos Fair, as the closest they have ever come to riding a horse in their lives. And need I point out that more than 86 percent of Argentines live in large cities? For most of our young people and children, the world of *Martín Fierro* is more alien than even the futuristic scenarios of Japanese comics.

Of course, this has a lot to do with globalization. From Bangkok to São Paulo, from Buenos Aires to Los Angeles or Sydney, young people listen to the same music, children watch the same cartoons, families get their clothes, food, and entertainment at the same chain stores; products and trade flow back and forth across increasingly penetrable national frontiers; mass media and tourism make different ideas, religions, and lifestyles more familiar.

But globalization is an ambiguous reality. Many factors purport to be leading us toward a breakdown of the cultural barriers that formerly prevented recognition of the common dignity of human beings, and toward an acceptance of the diversity of conditions, races, sex, and culture. Never before has mankind had such an opportunity to create a multifaceted, caring global community. And yet the indifference that exists with regard to our increasing social imbalances, the unilateral imposition of values and customs on the part of certain cultures, the ecology crisis, and the exclusion of millions of human beings from the benefits of development leave this issue open to serious debate. In this context, the creation of a caring, fraternal human family remains a utopia.

Real growth in mankind's conscience can only be founded on dialogue and love. Dialogue and love mean recognizing the differences of others, accepting diversity. Only then can we call it a true community: by not attempting to subject others to my criteria and priorities, by not "absorbing" others, but by recognizing them as valuable for what they are, and celebrating the diversity that is enriching for us all. Not to do so is narcissism, imperialism, plain foolishness.

This also applies in reverse: How can I maintain dialogue, how can I love, how can I build something if I let my potential input get diluted, lost, disappear? Globalization as a one-directional and uniformizing imposition of values, practices, and trade goes hand in hand with integration understood as being cultural, intellectual, and spiritual imitation and subordination. So we should be neither prophets of isolation, localist hermits in a global world, nor mindless and mimetic passengers trailing along in the caboose, admiring the fireworks of a World that belongs to others, all agape and applauding on cue. Different peoples, in joining the global dialogue, bring the values of their own culture and must defend them against any undue absorption or "laboratory synthesis" that might water them down into what is "the norm," what is "global." And—when they bring those values—they in turn receive the culture of other people, with the same respect and dignity.

Nor is there any room here for messy eclecticism, because then the values of a people become uprooted from the fertile soil that made them and sustains their being, and get mixed together as if in a junk shop, where "it's all the same, not to worry . . . we'll all end up 'down there' anyway."

The Nation as the continuity of a common history

We can benefit from our "national poem" only if we realize that what it narrates has to do with us directly, here and now; not because we are gauchos or wear a poncho, but because the drama that its author, José Hernández, narrates is set in the actual history that brought us to where we are today. The men and women reflected in the story lived in this land, and their decisions, work, and ideals shaped the reality that we form part of today, that affects us directly today. It is that very "productivity," those "effects," that capacity to be set in the real dynamic of history, that makes *Martín Fierro* a "national poem." Not the guitar, the *malón* (raid), and the *payada* (counterpoint singing).

And this is where an appeal to conscience is necessary. We Argentines have a dangerous tendency to think that

everything begins today, to forget that you don't get something for nothing, and that things don't just drop from the
sky. This in itself is a problem: unless we learn to recognize and accept the errors and successes of our past, which
gave rise to the good and bad of the present, we will be condemned to repeat them over and over again forever, which—
in fact—is not actually eternal, as the noose can only be
stretched so far . . . But there is more: if we sever our links
with the past, we'll be doing the same with our future. We
need to start looking at what is around us . . . and inside of
us. Wasn't there a negation of the future, a total lack of responsibility toward the future generations, in the flippancy
with which the institutions, assets, and even the people of
our country were treated?

One thing is certain: we are historical people. We live in
time and space. Every generation needs its predecessors, and
owes itself to its successors. And that, largely, is what being a
Nation means: understanding ourselves as a continuation of
the task of other men and women who already made their
contribution, and as builders of a common area, a dwelling,
for those who will follow us.

As "global" citizens, reading *Martín Fierro* can help bring us "down to earth" and curb this "globality" by acknowledging the struggles of the people who built our nationality, and making the journey as a nation our very own.

Being a nation means, above all, having an ethical attitude that springs from freedom

With the financial crisis, we are once again faced with this basic question: What is the underpinning of our so-called social ties? We say it so gravely at risk of being lost—but what exactly is it? What is it that "ties" me, that "binds" me to other people in a particular place, to the point where we share a common destiny?

Allow me to answer that: it is a matter of ethics. The basis of the connection between morality and social issues lies in that space (so elusive, by the way) in which man is a social being, a political animal, in the words of Aristotle and the classic republican tradition. It is man's social nature that underpins the possibility of a contract between free individuals, as proposed by the liberal democratic traditions (very often opposing traditions, as evidenced by numerous confrontations throughout our history). So presenting the crisis as a moral problem means we will have to refer back to the universal, human values that God sowed in man's heart and that ripen apace with our personal and collective growth. When we bishops keep saying, over and over again, that the crisis is fundamentally a moral crisis, we are not brandishing a cheap sense of morals, reducing the political, social, and economic issues to a matter of the individual's conscience. That would be "moralizing."

We are not "feathering our own nest" (since conscience and morals are, of course, Church matters); no, we are referring to the collective appraisals that have been expressed in historical, political, and social attitudes, actions, and processes.

The free-will actions of human beings, in addition to our own individual responsibility, have far-reaching consequences: they generate structures that endure over time and create a climate in which certain values can either occupy a central place in public life or be marginalized from the reigning culture. And this, too, falls within the moral sphere. That is why we must regain the particular way we had, in our history, of coexisting and forming a community. From this standpoint, let us now go to the poem. Like any popular story, *Martín Fierro* begins with a description of the "original paradise."

It depicts an idyllic reality in which the gaucho's life follows the serene pace of nature, surrounded by everything dear to him, working happily and skillfully, enjoying the company of his friends, and living a simple human lifestyle. What is the meaning of this scenario?

First of all, the author was not moved by a kind of nostalgia for a "gaucho lost Paradise." The literary device of describing an ideal situation at the beginning is no more than an initial presentation of the ideal itself. The value to be reflected is not behind us, at the "origin," but up ahead, in the project. At the origin is the dignity of a child of God, the vocation, the call to implement a project.

It is a matter of "putting the end at the beginning" (an idea which, by the way, is profoundly biblical and Christian). The direction in which we steer our coexistence has to do with the kind of society we want to be, with what our goal is. Therein lies the key to a nation's character. This does not mean we should ignore the biological, psychological, and psychosocial elements that influence our decisions. We cannot help but take up the burden (in the negative sense of constraints, conditioning, encumbrances, but also in the positive sense of carrying with us, incorporating, aggregating, integrating) of the inheritance received, the behaviors, preferences, and values that have been built up over time. However, a Christian perspective (and this is one of the things that Christianity has brought to mankind as a whole) values both "the given," what is immanent in man and cannot be otherwise, and what comes forth from his freedom, from his openness to all that is new; in short, from his transcendent spirit, always in accordance with the virtuality of "the given."

Now society's constraints and the form they took, as well as the discoveries and creations of the spirit in expanding human horizons always just a little bit further, along with the natural law innate in our conscience, come into play and are materialized in time and space: in a specific community, sharing a land, proposing common goals, building their own way of being humans, of cultivating the numerous ties, together, over many shared experiences, preferences, decisions, and events. That is what gives rise to a common ethic and openness toward a destiny of abundance that defines man as a spiritual being.

That common ethic, that "moral dimension," is what enables the group to grow together, without enmity. If we think of a pilgrimage, the act of starting out from the same place and heading for the same destination enables the column to continue as a unit, regardless of the different pace of each group or individual.

To sum up this idea, then, what is it that makes a bunch of people a nation? First of all, there is a natural law and then a heritage. Second, there is a psychological factor: man becomes man (each individual or the species as it evolves) through communication, interaction, love for his fellow beings. Through words and through love. And third, these biological and psychological-evolutionary factors become real and really come into play, in our free-will behavior, in the desire to bond with others in a certain way, to build our lives with our neighbors in a range of shared practices and preferences. (Saint Augustine defined a people as "an assemblage of reasonable beings bound together by a common agreement as to what they love.")

What is "natural" grows into what is "cultural" and "ethical"; the social instinct takes on human form in the free choice to become "us." A choice that, like all human actions, tends to become a habit (in the best sense of the word), generates a feeling of belonging, and gives rise to historical institutions, to the extent that each of us comes into this world within a community already formed (the family, the *patria*) without this curtailing the responsible freedom of each person. And all this rests solidly on the values that God imprinted on our human nature, on the divine breath that encourages us from within and that makes us children of God. That natural law that was gifted to us and imprinted on us so that it would "become consolidated down through the ages, and develop and grow with the passage of time" (see Vincent of Lérins, *Commonitory*, chapter 23). This natural law, which—throughout history and life—becomes consolidated, develops, and grows, is what saves us from the so-called relativism of consensus values. Values cannot be consensual: they just are.

In the accommodating game of "reaching a consensus on values" there is always the risk, predictably, of "downgrading." At that point, we are no longer building on solid ground, we are entering the violence of degradation. Somebody once said that our civilization is not just a throwaway civilization, it's also "biodegradable."

Getting back to our poem: *Martín Fierro* is not the Bible, of course, but it is a text in which, for various reasons, we Argentines see ourselves reflected. It is a medium for learning something about our history and for dreaming about our future:

I have known this land
in which my compatriot lived
and had his cabin
and his children and his wife.
It was a delight to see
how he spent his days.

This, then, is the "initial setting" in which the drama unfolds. *The Gaucho Martín Fierro* is, above all, an inclusionary poem. Everything will later be disrupted by some twist of fate, embodied by the judge, the mayor, and the colonel, among others. We suspect the conflict is not merely literary. What lies behind the text?

MARTÍN FIERRO, AN "INCLUSIONARY" POEM

A modern country, but a country for all

Rather than an abstract "epic poem," *Martín Fierro* is a poem of protest with a clear intention: to oppose the official government policy and propose that the gauchos be included in the newly developing country:

> *The poor man being stateless*
> *is fortune's wretched cast-off*
> *for no one takes his side*
> *in the defense of his race.*
> *The gaucho deserves home,*
> *school, church, and rights*

And Martín Fierro came to life, far more than the author intended, becoming the classic example of all those persecuted by an unjust, exclusionary system. The verses of the poem are impregnated with a certain folklore imbued from the surroundings, so Fierro touches not only on the desirability of promoting cheap labor, but also on man's dignity in his homeland, taking charge of his destiny through work, love, festivity, and fraternity.

From here, we can begin to take our reflections further. We want to know where to place our hope, how to rebuild the social ties so grievously affected in these times. The pot-banging protest was like a spark of self-defense, spontaneous and at a popular level (though to keep repeating it detracts from its original meaning).

We know it wasn't enough just to bang our pots and pans: what we need most now is something to put in them. We must regain, in an orderly and creative way, the prominence that we never should have relinquished, so we cannot now stick our head back in the sand and let our leaders do and undo as they wish. We cannot do that for two reasons: one, because we've seen what happens when political and economic power becomes detached from the people; and two, because the task of reconstruction belongs not just to some but to all of us, in the same way that Argentina consists not only of the ruling class, but of each and every one of us living on this part of the planet.

So, what then? I find the historical context of *Martín*

Fierro significant: a society taking form, a project that excludes a large sector of the population, sentencing it to statelessness and disappearance, and a proposal for inclusion. Are we not in a similar situation today? Haven't we suffered the consequences of a model of a country built around certain economic interests, that excludes majorities, generates poverty and marginalization, and that tolerates all kinds of corruption provided the interests of the hard-core power are left untouched? Haven't we been a part of that perverse system, partially accepting its principles as long as it wasn't dipping into our pockets, shutting our eyes to those who were being excluded and who were being bulldozed by injustice, until that injustice nearly drove us all out?

Now we have to draw up an economic and social program, yes, but one that is fundamentally a political project in the broadest sense of the term.

What kind of society do we want? *Martín Fierro* directs our gaze toward our vocation as a people, as a nation. The poem invites us to shape our desire for a society in which everyone has a place: the Buenos Aires merchant, the gaucho on the coast, the shepherd in the north, the craftsman of the northwest, the native, and the immigrant, and where none of them covets the whole thing for himself, driving the others from the land.

The gaucho must have schools . . .

Schools were, for decades, an important means of social and national integration. For the children of the gauchos, the migrants coming from the interior of the country in to the cities, and even the foreigners who disembarked on this land, basic education provided the elements that enabled them to transcend their origins and find a place in the construction of a common project.

Today, too, from the many enriching educational proposals, we must focus fully on education.

Over the last few years, and hand in hand with an idea of country that was no longer particularly concerned with including everyone and was not even capable of planning for the future, our educational system saw its prestige decline, its support and resources wane, and its place in the heart of society fade. The well-known catchphrase "school shopping" is not just a criticism of certain specific initiatives that we have witnessed; it brings up a whole concept, according to which society is nothing more than a market. It puts schooling on the same plane as any other lucrative venture. And we should remember, time and time again, that this was not the idea behind our educational system that helped to form, albeit with successes and failures, a national community.

In this respect, we Christians have, for centuries, undeniably contributed a great deal. I don't mean to get involved in controversy and differences of opinion that take a lot of energy. I simply want to draw everyone's attention, particularly the attention of Catholic teachers, to the extremely important task at hand.

Depreciated, undervalued, and even attacked by many, the daily task of everyone who keeps the schools going, in the face of all kinds of difficulties, with low salaries and giving much more than they receive, is still one of the best examples of what we have to focus on again: personal dedication to the project of a country for all. A project which, from the educational, religious, or social standpoint, is political in the highest sense of the word: the building of a community.

This political project of inclusion is the task not only of the governing party, or even of the ruling class as a whole; it belongs to all of us. The seeds for the "new era" are sown in the specific, everyday life of each of the nation's members, in each decision regarding one's neighbor, in accepting one's responsibilities, in small things and big things, and more so in the bosom of our families and in our everyday school or working life.

> *But God has to allow*
> *these things to improve*
> *though we must remember*
> *in order to do the job well*
> *that the fire, to provide heat,*
> *must always be lit underneath.*

But this calls for further reflection.

MARTÍN FIERRO, A COMPENDIUM OF CIVIC ETHICS

Hernández, too, probably realized that the "genuine" gauchos, the gauchos of flesh and blood, were not going to behave like "little English lords" in the "new society being forged."

Coming from another culture, used to the open spaces,

accustomed to decades of resistance and struggle, outsiders in a world that was springing up with very different parameters from their own, they, too, would have to make an enormous effort to integrate, once the doors were opened to them.

The resources of popular culture

The second part of our "national poem" claimed to be a kind of "handbook of civic virtues" for gauchos, a "key" to becoming integrated in the new nation.

> *And what I say*
> *you can all believe.*
> *So, therefore, understand me,*
> *I am not tainted by greed.*
> *It will not rain on the cabin*
> *where this book is read.*

Martín Fierro is full of the elements that Hernández himself had imbibed from the folklore, elements which, along with his defense of certain specific and immediate rights, quickly earned him great support. Moreover, in time,

generations upon generations of Argentines reread *Fierro* . . .
and rewrote it, adding to his words their own experiences of
struggle, expectations, searching, suffering . . . *Martín Fierro*
came to represent the determined, fraternal, justice-loving,
indomitable country. That is why it's still pertinent today.
That's why those "tips" on "taming" the gaucho far tran-
scended the meaning they had when written and are still
today a mirror of civic virtues that are not abstract but are
deeply embodied in our history. We shall now take a look at
those virtues and values.

The advice of *Martín Fierro*

I invite you to read this poem. Not just out of literary interest, but as a way of letting the wisdom of our people speak to
you, the wisdom that has been captured in this singular
work. Beyond the words, beyond the story, you will see that
what we are left with, beating inside us, is a kind of emotion,
a desire to twist the arm of all injustice and lies and to continue building a history of solidarity and fraternity, in a
common land where we can all grow as human beings;
a community where freedom is not an excuse to disregard

justice, where punishment is not meted out only on the poor, and where everybody has a place. I hope you feel the same as I do: that it isn't a book about the past, but rather about the future we can build. I am not going to extend this message— which is already very extensive—by going into the many values that Hernández puts in the mouth of Fierro and other characters in the poem. I simply invite you to consider them in depth, through reflection and, why not, through dialogue in each of our educational communities. Here I will set out only some of the many ideas we can recapture.

Honesty or "trickery": Acting truthfully and with goodness . . . or out of convenience

> *Man is born with the astuteness*
> *that has to serve him as his guide.*
> *Without it he would succumb,*
> *but in my experience*
> *in some it turns to good sense*
> *and in others to trickery.*
> *Some men's heads*

are full of knowledge;

wise men take many guises

but I, though unknowledgeable, say

that instead of learning a lot

it is better to learn what is good.

A starting-off point. "Honesty" or "trickery" as ways of organizing one's own gifts and acquired experience. Acting appropriately, in accordance with the truth and goodness that are possible here and now, as opposed to well-known manipulating information, situations, and interactions out of self-interest.

The mere accumulation of knowledge (for whatever purpose) or true wisdom, which includes "knowing" in the double sense of knowing and appreciating, and which is guided both by truth and goodness. "Everything is permissible for me, but not everything is beneficial for me," as Saint Paul would say. Why? Because, besides my needs, desires, and preferences, there are those of my neighbor; and what satisfies one at the expense of the other ends up destroying both.

The hierarchy of values and the success ethics of the "winner"

> *Neither fear nor greed*
> *is welcome if they rob one.*
> *So do not fret*
> *over perishable things.*
> *Never be generous to the rich*
> *and never be mean to the poor.*

Far from suggesting that we be contemptuous of material things as such, the popular wisdom expressed in these words considers perishable goods as a means to an end, as a way to reach a higher level. That's why it says not to be generous to the rich (the type of calculating, servile behavior that would be recommended by the "trickery" of Old Vizcacha) and not to be mean to the poor (who do need us and, according to the Gospel, have nothing with which to repay us). Human society cannot be governed by a "law of the jungle" by which everyone tries to snatch what he can, at any cost. And we know, only too painfully, that there is no "automatic" mechanism for ensuring fairness and justice. Only an ethical choice transformed into specific practices, with effective means, is capable of preventing man from falling prey to man. But this is the same as postulating an order of values that is more important than personal gain and, therefore, a type of asset that is superior to tangible ones. And we are not talking about issues that require a certain religious belief in order to be understood; we are talking about principles such as human dignity, solidarity, and love.

> *"You call me 'teacher' and 'master,' and rightly so, for indeed I am. If I, therefore, the master and teacher, have washed your feet, you ought to wash one another's feet. I have given you a model to follow, so that as I have done for you, you should also do."*
>
> JOHN 13:13–15

A community that does not bow down before wealth, success, and prestige and that is capable, instead, of washing the feet of the poor and needy would be more in keeping with this teaching than the winner-at-any-cost ethic that has been so unfortunately prevalent in recent times.

Work and the kind of person we want to be

We are obliged to work
because we have to spend.
Don't risk suffering
a sorry situation.
The heart of a man who is forced to beg
bleeds profusely.

Do we need to add anything here? History has branded our people with a sense of the dignity of work and the worker. Is there anything more humiliating than not being able to earn a living? Is there a worse way to proclaim the uselessness and nonexistence of a human being? Can a society that condones such baseness while shielding itself behind abstract technical explanations light the way for man's self-realization?

But our recognition of this, which we all proclaim, isn't fully cooked. Not just because of the objective conditions that are responsible for the terrible unemployment at present (conditions which, we must not keep quiet about it, have their origin in a way of organizing coexistence that places profit above justice and law), but also because of a mentality of *viveza* (another local term!)—"craftiness"—that has become a part of our culture. "Getting away with things" . . . in the easiest way possible. "Money makes money" . . . "nobody ever got rich by working" . . . beliefs that have nurtured a culture of corruption which undoubtedly has to do with the "shortcuts" by which many have tried to circumvent the law of earning one's living by the sweat of one's brow.

Urgent care for the weakest

When the stork gets old
its sight fails, and
in its old age it is cared for
by all its young daughters.
Learn from the storks
this example of tenderness.

According to the "winner" ethic, whatever is considered useless gets thrown out. This is the "throwaway" civilization. In the ethics of a truly humane community, in the country that we would like to have and that we can build, every human being is valuable, and the elderly are valuable in their own way, for many reasons: the duty of filial respect, set out in the Ten Commandments; the indubitable right to rest within their community, earned by those who have lived, suffered, and contributed what they could; the contribution that only they can still make to their society, since, as Martín Fierro himself says, *"it is out of the mouths of the old / that the truth is spoken."*

We should not wait until the social security system, currently ruined by the pillaging that has gone on, gets back on its feet; there are countless ways in which we can provide a service to our seniors; in the meantime, all we need is goodwill and some creativity. Similarly, we cannot ignore the specific possibilities to do something to help the children and all those who are sick and suffering. The belief that there are "structural" issues involving society as a whole and the state itself, in no way exempts us from doing our bit, however small it may be.

No more theft, bribery, or "don't get involved"

The bird with the hooked beak
is fond of thieving.

but the thinking man
never takes a cent,
for while there is no shame in poverty
there is in theft.

This may be one of the country's most ill-learned lessons. But beyond that, apart from never again permitting or justifying theft and bribery, we would have to take far more decisive and more positive action. For example, by asking ourselves not only what we should not take from others, but rather what we can give. How can we express the idea that there is also "shame" in indifference, individualism, withholding (stealing) what one can contribute to society just for the sake of "doing my thing"?

But because [the doctor of law] wished to justify himself,
he said to Jesus, "And who is my neighbor?" Jesus replied,
"A man fell victim to robbers as he went down from
Jerusalem to Jericho. They stripped and beat him and
went off leaving him half-dead. A priest happened to be
going down that road, but when he saw him, he passed
by on the opposite side. Likewise a Levite came to the
place, and when he saw him, he passed by on the

opposite side. But a Samaritan traveler who came upon
him was moved with compassion at the sight. He
approached the victim, poured oil and wine over his
wounds and bandaged them. Then he lifted him up on
his own animal, took him to an inn and cared for him.
The next day he took out two silver coins and gave them
to the innkeeper with the instruction, 'Take care of him.
If you spend more than what I have given you, I shall
repay you on my way back.' Which of these three, in your
opinion, was neighbor to the robbers' victim?" He
answered, "The one who treated him with mercy." Jesus
said to him, "Go and do likewise."

LUKE 10:29–37

Empty words, true words

Try, if you are singers,
to sing with feeling.
Do not tune your instrument
just for the sake of talking,
and make a habit of singing
about things that matter.

Communication, hypercommunication, noncommunication. How many "superfluous" words are spoken among us? How much gossip, defamation, and slander is there? How much superficiality, banality, and wasted time? The ability to communicate ideas and feelings is a wonderful gift we don't fully appreciate.

Couldn't we make an effort to stop all the "gabbing" we do "just for the sake of it"? Might that make us more attentive to what we say too much of and what we say too little of, especially those of us whose mission is to teach, speak, and communicate?

WORDS AND FRIENDSHIP

Finally, let us talk about the stanza that so clearly reflects the commandment of love in difficult circumstances for our country. The verse has become a slogan, a platform, a rallying cry, and we should recall it again and again:

Brothers must stand united,
for that is the primal law.
They must stand truly united

at all times,
for if they fight amongst themselves
outsiders will devour them.

This is a critical time for our *patria*. Critical and founda-
tional, and, for that very reason, brimming with hope. Hope
is as removed from effortlessness as it is from fainthearted-
ness. It demands that we give our best to the task of rebuild-
ing what is communal to us, what makes us a people.

These reflections are intended only to awaken a desire:
that of getting down to work, encouraged and enlightened
by our own history, of not letting go of our dream of a *patria*
of brothers, which guided so many men and women in
this land.

What will future generations say of us? Can we face
the challenges before us? The answer is: Why not? Without
pomp or messianic illusions, or impossible certainties; it's a
matter of plunging bravely back into our ideals, the ones that
guided our history, and of starting, right now, to implement
other possibilities, other values, other forms of behavior.

In summary, here is the last verse I quote from *Martín*

Fierro, a verse that Hernández puts in the mouth of the gaucho's eldest son in his bitter reflection on jail:

> *Since of all the things,*
> *as far as I, in my ignorance, understand,*
> *that His Divine Majesty*
> *granted to arrogant man*
> *speech is the first,*
> *and the second is friendship.*

Words or speech allow us to communicate, connect us, enabling us to share ideas and feelings, provided we speak the truth always, without exception. Friendship, including social friendship, with its "long arm" of justice, which is the greatest treasure, the asset which cannot be sacrificed for any other, which must be nurtured above all else.

Words and friendship. "And the Word became flesh and made his dwelling among us" (John 1:14). He did not set himself apart from us; he became our friend.

> *"No one has greater love than this, to lay down one's life*
> *for one's friends. You are my friends if you do what I*

command you. I no longer call you slaves, because a slave does not know what his master is doing. I have called you friends, because I have told you everything I have heard from my Father."

JOHN 15:13–15

If we start, right now, to value these two gifts, our country's history could be very different.

Let us end by placing these wishes in the hands of the Lord with the prayer for our *patria* offered up by the Argentine bishops:

Jesus Christ, Lord of history, we are in need of thee.
We are wounded and overwhelmed.
We need thy comfort and thy strength.
We want to be a nation,
a nation identified by its passion for truth
and its commitment to the common good.

Give us the courage of the freedom of God's children,
to love all people, to the exclusion of none,
favoring the poor and forgiving those who offend us,
scorning hatred and building peace.

Grant us the wisdom of dialogue and the

joy of hope that thwarts us not.

Thou hast summoned us. We are here, Lord,

close to Mary,

who hails us from Lujan, thus:

Argentina! Sing out and walk boldly on!

Jesus Christ, Lord of history, we are in need of thee.

Amen.

ABOUT THE AUTHORS

Sergio Rubin, an award-winning author and journalist, is currently chief of religious news for the Argentinian newspaper *Clarín* and editor of its supplement *Valores Religiosos* (Religious Values). He covered more than a dozen of Pope John Paul II's trips, his funeral, and the election of Pope Benedict XVI. Among many international figures, he interviewed Mother Teresa.

Francesca Ambrogetti, a journalist and social psychologist, currently teaches journalism. In 1982, she headed the Association for Foreign Press in Argentina and, from 2000 to 2003, the Association of Foreign Correspondents. She collaborates with international media such as Vatican Radio.